SEEING THE WOOD AND THE TREES

THE DEANLAND POEMS

Doris Eastman

Copyright © 2017 Doris Eastman

All rights reserved.

ISBN:1547092734
ISBN-13: 978-1547092734

Doris moved to Deanland Wood Park
in 1992 and soon after, began to submit poems for
publication in the Park's bi-monthly magazine.

This anthology of the poems is in celebration
of the author's **100th** birthday in July 2017.

DONATION

This book has been compiled in secret –
as a present for Doris' 100th birthday.
If, through sales, a profit is made, the
money will be given to a charity – to be
chosen by Doris (when she finds out!)

ACKNOWLEDGMENTS

Stephen and Gill Eastman compiled Doris' poems into this format; arranged the printing, proof reading etc, so if you spot errors, they are Stephen and Gill's, rather than Doris'. Thanks are due to Jennie in the Estate Office who made the *News* archive available to Stephen so that both the poems and articles could be scanned for this edition.

Timeline for Doris' *Deanland News* Poems

Year	Month	Title	Page
1993	10	Guessing in the Garden	3
	12	Christmas Past & Present	
1994	2	Deanland Poem	6
	8	Old Tyme Night	
	10	Autumn	
1995	2	Tender Seedlings	9
	6	Hello Summer	
	8	Old Tyme Night	
	12	Sheepish Tale	
1996	2	1996 & All That	15
	10	I Love Summer	
	12	Christmas	
1997	2	Happy New Year	19
	4	Welcome Back	
	12	Christmas	
1998	8	Something About Deanld	21
	12	All the Jolly	
1999	4	Spring Song	23
	6	It's a Gift	
	10	Autumn Avenue	
	12	Christmas 1999	

Other items included from *Deanland News* are from the period of the poem.

Timeline for Doris' *Deanland News* Poems

Year	M	Title	Page
2000	2	Goings & Comings	29
	4	Into Spring	
	6	Summer's Here	
	10	Into Autumn	
	12	Can It Be	
2001	2	Such a Thing	35
	4	It's Nice	
	12	Not Only	
2002	4	Hurrah for Spring	40
	6	Moon in June	
	8	Not Lately	
	10	As the Case May Be	
	12	More About Emily	
2003	2	To 2003	46
	2	Springtime Stroll	
	6	Memory Lane	
	8	In Praise of Deanland	
	10	The Flower of Friendship	
2004	2	2004	52
	4	Something About Spring	
	6	End of a Perfect Day	
	8	Looking Back	
	10	A Pleasant Outing	
	12	Festive Fancies	
2005	2	To 2005	62
	4	Here Again	
	6	It's Back	
	8	Made of This	
	10	But Not Goodbye	
	12	The Spirit of Christmas	

Timeline for Doris' *Deanland News* Poems

Year	Month	Title	Page
2006	2	I Wonder	70
	4	All in The Air	
	6	Such a Garden	
	8	Enjoy	
	10	Spoilt For Choice	
	12	Just Thinking	
2007	2	The Gate of the Year	76
	6	Guessing in the Garden	
	8	Nonagenarian Notions	
	10	A Lovely Day	
	12	Vera	
2008	4	Memories	81
	6	You See?	
	8	The Flower of Friendship	
	10	Dream-Stream	
	12	Jolly Holly-Days	
2009	2	Merry Musings	86
	4	Just The Thing	
	6	Morning Stroll	
	8	A Nice Day	
	10	Worth the Search	
	12	That Time Again	
2010	2	Sounds Good to Me	94
	4	It's Spring You See	
	6	Scientifically Proven	
	8	So Nice	
	10	Slippery Sam	
	12	The Hamper	

Timeline for Doris' *Deanland News* Poems

Year	M	Title	Page
2011	2	Meg's Choice	105
	4	Love Was There	
	6	Nice 'n Easy	
	8	Eventide	
	10	A Whisper of Whimsey	
	12	Always	
2012	2	This and That	112
	4	Why Just Dream	
	6	Jolly Fine Show	
	8	A Lakeside Lyric	
	10	A Bit Batty	
	12	The Cloak	
2013	2	Oh Blow!	120
	4	Seasonal Solilioquay	
	6	Is It	
	8	Idle Idyll	
	10	Artistic License	
	12	That Day Again	
2014	2	Sing a Song	126
	4	The Cup Winner	
	6	Tomorrow Sounds Good	
	8	Keep On Keeping Fit	
	10	So The Day	
	12	Santa For Ever	
2015	2	The Birdsong Was Sweet	132
	4	And I Am	
	6	Will You?	
	8	To Be Frank	
	10	Fares Please.	
	12	Oh and Ho Ho Ho	

Timeline for Doris' *Deanland News* Poems

Year	Month	Title	Page
2016	2	Blind Date	139
	4	Oh Mave	
	6	Just Jess	
	8	So It's Summer	
	10	Frown	
	12	Seasonal Greetings	
2017	2	Dream On	146
	4	Springs to Mind	
	6	Pensive Peggy	

DEANLAND *News*

- INFORMATION DESK
- SOCIAL CALENDAR
- PARK NEWS
- DEANLAND ESTATES

DEANLAND

PARK HOMES

PARK HOMES ESTATE

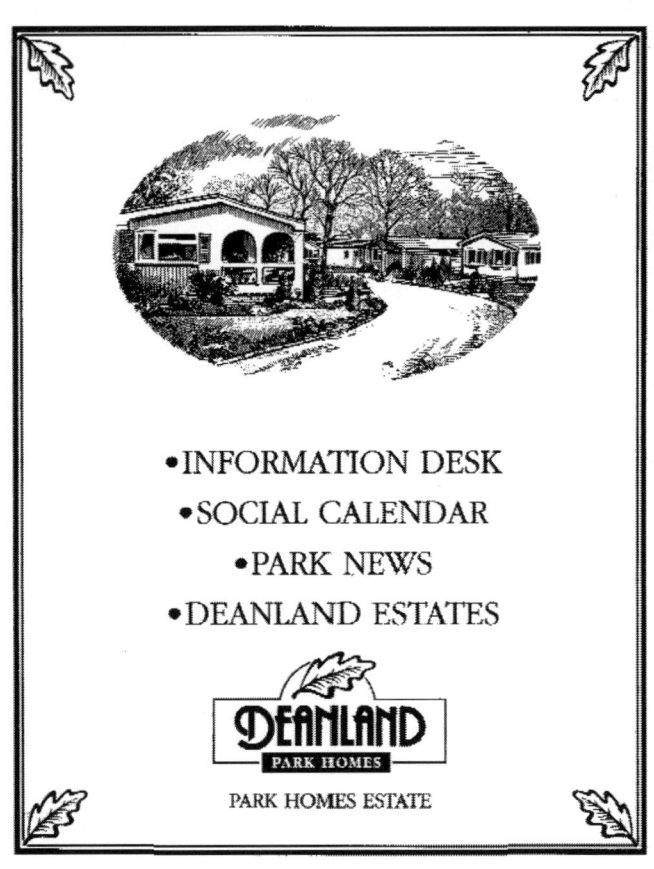

1993 cover

FOREWORD

Doris and Jim were married for 52 years. During that half-century, they had a variety business of ventures from running their own plumbing firm (Jim's skill) to pub landlords. They took over their first pub in 1966 – The Horse & Groom at Rushlake Green.

Whatever the enterprise, Doris was in charge of the administration, having been trained as a shorthand secretary with years of experience in the City of London. Perhaps due to this, or perhaps due to her love of reading novels, Doris has always been confident with words - very useful for writing poems, and winning at Scrabble.

Jim died early in 1992 and by the autumn of that year, Doris had moved into her newly renovated Park Home.

As many widows will attest, it is not just the bereavement that has to be overcome, but also the sheer fact of living alone. Doris' solution was to join some of the many Deanland groups – Ramblers, Singers, Entertainers, Keep Fit, Scrabble, Bingo, Coffee Mornings and Darts (she was captain of the women's team at their pub). The route from her home to the Social Centre became a well-trodden path.

With so many activities, Doris did not return to her writing until the following year. Her first *Deanland News* poem was in the October 1993 edition. Poems would appear three or four times in the early years, then by the millennium they were a regular feature. Doris' poems have been in just about every edition of the *News* since.

Although the poems were not written with the aim of a 'collection', we, her family, thought it would be a fitting tribute to all the hours Doris has spent honing her skill. We hope you enjoy them.

Back cover of the *News* during the 1990s.

INTRODUCTION

Deanland Wood Park has changed considerably since Doris moved here in 1992. To illustrate both this, and the diverse activities of residents, sample pages and items have been included to match the timing of the poems.

To set the scene, we have included some *News* pages that, we think, shed light on the Park and the way it is run.

In 2010, one of the founders of the Park, Hyman (Sidney) Wolek, the Father of the family owners of Deanland, died. In the June edition, Keith Whitehead, who was managing the park at that time, included an obituary and history of the family's involvement with Deanland.

He began by explaining that by 1954 the family had acquired two holiday caravans at Pegwell Bay, near Ramsgate, when Sidney and Joyce fancied a caravan park of their own. The search began....

In 1954, Sidney and Joyce sold their house in Orpington and bought Deanland Wood Park, at Golden Cross. Their life started at Deanland Wood Park living in a caravan with Nigel as a baby, Richard just leaving school helped with the new venture and eventually in 1968 with his young family emigrated to Australia, where they remain to this day. In 1963 Keith joined Sidney and Joyce as "Park Manager". By 1976 Sidney and Joyce emigrated to Spain to spend their retirement in the sun and sangria country, leaving the Park business to be run by Keith, Tanya and Nigel.

Sidney was a Freemason, joining a London Lodge in 1966, then to become the first joining member of Hamelsham Lodge, which meets at Herstmonceux. In Spain Sidney helped found a Spanish Freemasons Lodge under the Spanish constitution, raising much charity money. He also founded a Lions Club in Nerja Southern Spain, which raised large sums of charity money from the ex-pats. living there, they provided the first ambulance for the town of Nerja.

During the period in Spain, Sidney was invited to become a Freeman of the City of London, which remained until his death.

Nearly thirty years later they returned to live back in England, as Joyce's health was not too good. Joyce ended up being cared for in a Nursing home suffering with Dementia, where she still remains.

Sidney spent a lot of time at the Park enjoying its facilities and becoming well liked by its residents, and was regularly seen riding around the Park in his blue buggy.

Sidney fell ill before last Christmas, recovered in hospital, returned home only to fall ill again on 23 March eventually dying in hospital on the 3 April 2010 at the grand old age of 94.

Deanland Wood Park is still owned by the children, with the next generation, Keith's son Stephen as Park Manager, history seems to be repeating itself!

So we say farewell to Sidney/Dad a well liked Father and friend to the Park, who lived a good long life and with his wife, Joyce, founded one of the best Park Home Estates in the Country.

Just to dispel any rumours that may be going around the Park following Dad's death: **The family is not selling The Park; nothing is changing for the present.** Our Mother, who is 90 this year, is still alive, albeit in a nursing home, so we need to consider her and she could live to be a hundred!

Keith Whitehead

[A 2010 rumour would turn out to be more than that six years later.]

We now head back to the beginning of Doris' Deanland experience - 1993.

DEANLAND

AUG/SEPT 1993

Well ... is the recession nearly over? I think it might be, we are receiving many more enquiries and selling more homes than we have done for the last three years. But ... prices have to be realistic, it is a buyers market out there and we are not immune from that. We have made our prices so competative and the Park is looking fantastic, that a buyer just has to settle with us. It is so promising that the start of BADGERS WALK is going to happen this Winter, with the first homes being occupied in the Spring of 1994.

BADGERS WALK has been priced to sell the first phase quickly, so there has never been a better time to buy a new Park Home at DEANLAND WOOD PARK, with a garage on a brand new area. Prices are bound to rise as this recession fades away.

During August will see the arrival of Natural Gas in the pipes, and homes beginning to be connected up. This is another milestone for the Park, for when we first acquired Deanland in 1951, there was only an electic system of sorts, no other services. Look how far we have come!

The whole Park is looking lovely, and that is thanks mainly to all you keen gardeners, who lovingly tend your gardens, and all the rain we have had. Talking about rain, when are we going to see our Summer! Maybe we had it last Wednesday week!

The Park has been entered in the "Best Kept Village Competition" and is representing the local villages of Ripe and Chalvington on its own. We wait for the results with baited breath.

Do not get burned in the Sun, if it comes!

Keith Whitehead

OPINION

Recession? – Have we been here before?

Doris' Deanland Poems

DEANLAND
OCT~~NOV '93

Another milestone in the history of DEANLAND WOOD PARK was reached at the end of September this year when the first home was connected to NATURAL GAS. When you think, it has taken so many years to arrive at this point, that its arrival is a little bit uncanny. Some ten years ago I first enquired of the then Gas Board if they would consider bringing the main to our Park. The answer was "no", too far, not worth it, was the reason given. Remember at that time the Gas Board was a public utility subsidised by the Government. Today, under the heading of BRITISH GAS, and a Company responsible to its shareholders, it finds it more than worthwhile to supply Deanland with Natural Gas. However it is not without its costs, tempers have been frayed, water mains fractured and what about the mess! Hopefully the disruption to the Park is getting less and I hope you will all agree it has been worth it. I take this opportunity to apologise to you all for the mess, disruption to the water supply and the aggravation of not being able to easily drive around the Park together with the damage to gardens etc. I also thank you all for your tolerance and understanding, the vast majority of you are taking it in your stride. This just goes to prove the type of folk we have living here at DEANLAND PARK. It probably would not have been so well understood elsewhere. Thank you all.

We are fast approaching a very beautiful time of the year for all those living here at DEANLAND WOOD PARK, the Autumn, a time when the trees change their colour and the days become cooler. Every season has its own attraction when you live in the country.

This August saw our Annual Fete reach new heights of excellence, a wonderful time was had by all. My thanks, and I know yours to my Father, Sidney Wolek for being a fine "announcer" on the microphone, and to the Social Centre committee for all their hard work in making the day a success. The list of Garden Competition winners is featured later on in this edition.

There is new SHOW HOME available for viewing, it is the new Omar Southdown Tudor, and represents a typical 1994 model that can feel at home in BADGERS WALK as well as the PARK as a whole.

The work on BADGERS WALK has started in earnest, and is already taking shape. This is going to be a fantastic new area of the Park, with gentle bends on the roads and lovely oak trees. I cannot wait until MARCH '94 when the first homes will be occupied and DEANLAND WOOD PARK goes into another new and exiting phase.

KEITH WHITEHEAD

The first *News* edition to include a Doris Eastman poem.

My Top 10 Poems

Page	Title

Other Notes/Comments

1993 - 1999

BADGERS WALK

The roads are now in and the base course tarmac in place. It does look nice, it is going to be a lovely new area. We are on target for opening with the first homes on 1st March 1994. The first phase is 35 homes with half already spoken for.

St Wilfrid's Hospice respond to residents' charitable giving.

2 MILL GAP ROAD, EASTBOURNE, EAST SUSSEX BN21 2HJ
(0323) 644500 Hospice
Tel: (0323) 642006 Office
(0323) 642056 Office
Secretary: Brian Hampson

6 July 1993

Mrs F Kellie
Beech Avenue
Deanland Wood
Golden Cross
HAILSHAM/E Sussex
BN27 3SR

Dear Mrs Kellie

We were absolutely delighted to receive once more the proceeds from your annual Coffee Morning.

On behalf of our Chairman, Councillor Dennis P Cullen and all the Trustees, I should like to thank you most sincerely for donating the splendid amount of £1,054.36 towards the Hospice funds.

We greatly appreciate your continued interest and support, which is so encouraging to us all, who are connected with St Wilfrid's.

With our very good wishes
Yours sincerely

Michael D Willis
Bursar

GUESSING IN THE GARDEN

Have you ever heard the ringing of a Canterbury bell?
Or really seen a primrose looking prim?
Do hydrangeas go in hiding when the gardener comes along?
And tulips move their lips to speak to him?

Do carnations need a licence?
Rhododendrons look both ways?
Is Virginia creeper something one should shun?
Are lettuces permissive?
Why is fuchsia here today?
Maybe I'm suffering from too much sun.

Are lilies roses' sisters?
Honeysuckle really sweet?
Are wallflowers coy?
Do weeping willows cry?
It's a proper posy poser
And it's almost got me beet.
But I'll raise some bloomin' answers - if I try.

Why is Lizzie always busy?
Do cauliflowers bark?
There is no need to 'spur' me on,
It really is a 'lark'.

Are tiger-lilies dangerous?
Does red-hot-poker burn?
You must admit, it's really quite a farce.
It's very plain to see I have an awful lot to learn.
You'll 'dig' I'm due for 'putting out to grass'.

Hoe dear   Thistle do!!   Closing thyme!!!

CHRISTMAS, - PAST AND PRESENT

So many Christmases I've seen,
So many yuletides known.
So many crowded memories
Of festive days, long gone.

When I was young, and in my prime,
(believe me, there was such a time.)
The 'east-end' was my domicile,
And Christmas held a special style.

Bright coal-fires; pasted paper-chains.
Tan-sad scooters; wind-up trains.
Stilts; lead-soldiers; humming-tops; Meccano..
Rousing songs round the piano.

Street vendors, clamouring their wares,
Bright in the light of naphtha flares.
Jack Payne's band on the gramophone.
King George the fifth upon the throne.

Ten yards away, a railway-track.
Factories looming at the back.
In the street, horse-&-cart and tram.
(I'm 'freeing the cat' how old I am!)

The years have sped; as is their way,
And, with luck, on this Christmas day,
I'll be in Deanland, where the scene
Is panoramic and serene.

Instead of trams and factories,
Bright-eyed squirrels scale the trees.
No 'cat's-whiskers' and his master's voice,
Now in 'telly' and video we rejoice.

Santa, though, still shows his face,
Despite the dearth of chimney-space,
And, in the superstore Christmas grotto
'Business as usual' is his motto.

He greets the children by their names,
Whilst promising computer games.
For Christmas magic still, to them,
Is Santa-Claus, - and Bethlehem.

There is no doubt the change is good.
From grimy street, - to stream and wood.
Yet, in my heart, they both hold sway.

Here's to a Happy Christmas Day,

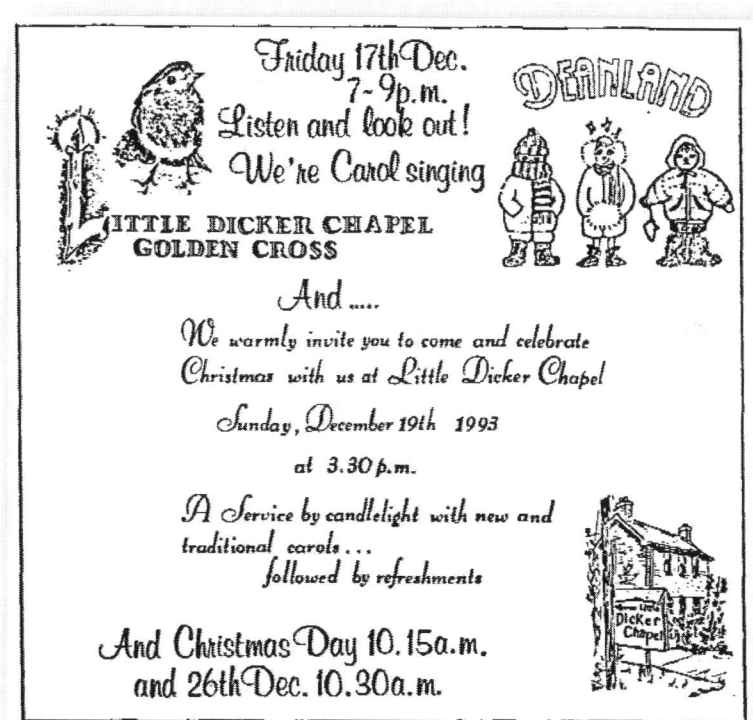

DEANLAND

There's a pleasing place I know
Deep in the Sussex Weald,
Where flowers in abundance grow
Midst trees and stream and field.

It's not far from the 'madding crowd',
Scarce half-a-hand of miles.
Just far enough to feel our space,
Just room to stretch our smiles.

A sense of welcome in the air
That makes one happy to be there.
People who greet one with a smile,
And seem prepared to chat.
To swop opinions for a while
And ponder this and that.

A caring, kind community,
Mainly retired, yet still
Pursuing hobbies, sport and games
With real panache and skill.

The varied social calendar
Has 'Welcome' on the mat.
It's there for one to take or leave.
Who could improve on that?
And - with pool, tavern, store and bus,
All one can say is "Lucky Us!"

I'm glad I found you, Deanland,
Though sorrow led me to you.
Whatever future's left to me
Can only prosper, through you.

JUNE & JULY 1994

JUNE 6th 1944 was D-Day, and the landings in Normandy, France, by the Allied Armies, was the beginning of the end of the last war. DEANLAND WOOD PARK sits on part of an ADVANCED LANDING GROUND that was built especially for the invasion into Europe. It was from here and other R.A.F. airfields and advanced landing grounds in the south, that air cover was given to those landings. In fact the first Spitfire air cover over the beaches was claimed to have come from DEANLAND A.L.G. Deanland was also uncomfortably placed on the route the V-1 rocket bomb (doodlebug) took to London, and the SPITFIRES from here were invaluable at shooting down these bombs. This was known as "diver duties" as the only way to get up enough speed to catch the rocket propelled bomb was to get well above it and dive at great speed and shoot it down. You had to be careful you did not get too close, otherwise you went down as well!

On the weekend of June 4th and 5th, we are holding a tribute to the months in 1944 that DEANLAND was an ADVANCED LANDING GROUND. There will be a static full sized Spitfire on display together with a "doodlebug". A SPITFIRE of 1943 will give an air display, weather permitting, on both Saturday and Sunday. There will also be displays of period military vehicles over the weekend. On Saturday night in the TAVERN will be a 1940's DANCE to a big band making the "Glen Miller Sound" admission is £7.50 and food of the period will be available. All welcome. Tickets for the dance are limited and available at the Office or the Tavern.

We have commissioned a painting depicting "Deanland at War" as a reminder of the role DEANLAND WOOD PARK played during that turning point in the last war. Limited edition prints will be sold during the weekend, at a special low price for those who want them.

This weekend is a TRIBUTE to those brave pilots and support men and women on this 50th Anniversary of D-Day. Please give us your support on any part of the weekend you can.

Keith Whitehead

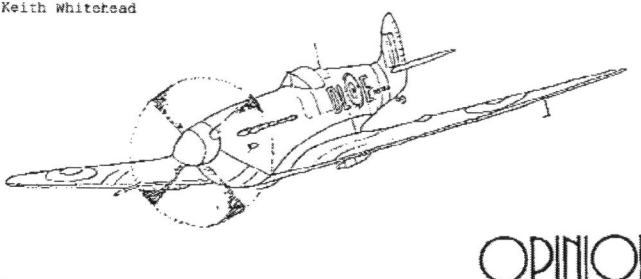

OPINION

AUTUMN

Softly sweet summer draws away,
And autumn takes the stage,
In robes of russet, green and gold,
And myriad shades of beige.

The swimming-pool is covered o'er;
It's served us all so well.
Content, it bides until once more
We languor in its spell.

Our light apparel stowed away,
We make our preparation
For those pursuits which autumn suits
In quiet anticipation.

For every season has its joy;
Each time of year its pleasure;
And, here in Deanland, we employ
Those charms in fullest measure.

May falling leaves and temperatures
Rest lightly on your mind,
For nature's calendar ensures
Spring won't be _far_ behind.

TO TENDER SEEDLINGS   1995

Too soon; through frosted earth,
Are bolder seedlings thrusting.
Beware, thou tender plants, and bide awhile.
Though you are anxious to appear,
And our hearts thrill to see you here,
Be not too trusting.
Place not your simple faith in nature's oft-times
                                fickle guile.

Be not diverted by that fitful sunshine
That sheds its radiance, then fades away.
Stay sheltered, and appreciate
That as beneath the soil you wait
So splendor will be added to your ultimate display.

And vey soon; you'll find it's true;
The warming soil will nurture you,
And play its part in nature's endless story.
And Oh, the joy that there will be
When you are there for us to see,
Proudly fulfilled, in all your brilliant glory.

ARRIVING EARLY APRIL

SHOW HOME Welcome

45' x 20' DEANLAND COTTAGE BY OMAR

This beautiful Park Home, especially designed for Deanland, with a warm country cottage feel about it, includes many choices of carpets, kitchens, curtains and furniture, even style of windows at no extra cost!

Our 'Deanland Package' price also includes a private driveway, with a 20ft garage, real brick skirting, two sets of brick steps and your garden laid with turf.

All for £76,000   (Summer 1995 Price)
 (Approx)

* *

DEANLAND 'ASTORIA' (SOCIAL CENTRE)

Wednesday 15th February

Of all the classic animated features in the incomparable Disney Library, one film stands apart - for it's bold experimentation and artistic achievements in capturing the drama, beauty and natural realism of forest life. That film is "BAMBI" Walt Disney's masterpiece.

The story of BAMBI traces the natural cycle of a young deer from birth and adolescence up through the birth of his own two fawns. As the story unfolds, Bambi learns the meaning of MAN and how all animals fear him. This film is PURE MAGIC.

Wednesday 22nd March

This month we are showing a much requested real classic film "THE AFRICAN QUEEN" with Katharine Hepburn and Humphrey Bogart. Superb combination of Bogart, who won an Oscar and spinster Hepburn downriver in Africa combating the elements, the Germans, and each other. Gorgeously filmed on location in the Belgian Congo.

Wonderful films that never fade.

Peggy & Ray.

* *

HELLO SUMMER

Hello Summer – welcome back.
You've been away too long.
We need your warmth to lift our hearts
And keep our spirits strong.
We've known the wonder of the Spring,
And that held charms indeed,
But, oh, the joy that Summer brings
Is what we sorely need.
Exalting in your warm embrace;
Your brilliant floral train.
Summer - You've been away too long,
So, - <u>welcome back</u> again.

'OLDE TYME' NIGHT

So many things are organised for Deanlanders' delight,
That, to acclaim them, one is spoilt for choice.
But, even so, I really think our recent 'Olde Tyme' Night
More than deserves that praise should raise its voice.

For, it was FUN – that is the word for it,
And everyone enjoyed it, so they tell,
And everybody played their part in swinging it along,
And, what is more, they DRESSED the part as well.

And there was music all the way, playing our favourite tunes.
Organ, piano, violin, clarinet and spoons.
And 'TURNS' and singers, even a Magician held us in his spell.

So, really there's no need to explain,
The verdict; on the evening is just that it was SWELL
  - and -
Wouldn't it be lovely if we did the same again?

A SHEEPISH TALE

Rising the other morning, scarce fully roused from sleep,
Drawing the blind, what do I find? - A garden full of sheep.

Well- it's only a little garden, and of sheep there were but two,
But - little garden, two big sheep
I call that full - don't you?

I looked at them, and they at me
All in a sort of daze.
They were where they should never be
The remedy was plain to see.
There certainly would have to be a parting of the ways.

They'd trampled on the helpless flowers
And eaten as they pleased.
Probably been doing so for hours.
I really felt quite 'cheesed'.

"Shoo", I said, and waved my arms,
That didn't do much good.
They looked at me impassively and stood fast where they stood.

I really felt quite sheepish,
More sheepish, perhaps than they.
I really didn't want them there,
But they seemed keen to stay.

I rang for Dave to help me out,
The early hour despite.
He understood, and was most kind,
Said he really didn't mind,
And would soon put matters right.

By the time that Dave arrived
The sheep had gone away.
We thought that was the end of it, and things would be OK.
But those two sheep thought otherwise,
And they were back - next day.

The farmer's sealed the gap now, though,
So I can freely sleep,
With easy mind - and leave behind
Rehearsals of 'Bo-Peep'.

DEANLAND BOWLS CLUB

Deanland Bowls Club cordially invite you to the Opening of our Practice Green on Saturday, 3rd August at 2.30pm for 3.00pm. Keith Whitehead has kindly consented to conduct the Opening Ceremony, which will be followed by a 'Spoon Drive'. To the uninitiated 'A Spoon Drive' is a competition in which all the Club Members compete for engraved spoons (donated by Morris Jeffers of Badgers Walk - nice one Morris). The spoons will be presented by Keith on completion of the competition. Remember to bring your own chairs.

The Competition will be followed by a Barbecue in the Tavern, tickets £3.50 available from the Tavern or from me at 20 Tall Timbers. There will be a Social/Get Together in the Tavern in the evening. Live music, not disco, by courtesy of Bill (thanks Bill), a Singalong and Raffle. Come and along and do your own thing.

Please support us and have fun at the same time. Raffle prizes gratefully accepted, to me please, to be drawn in the evening at the Social.

Pat Morris
Hon. Sec. Deanland B

Best Village Shop in Wealden 1996

Commendation

This is to certify that

Mr and Mrs Gambrell

of

Deanland Stores, Deanland Park,

Golden Cross

were runners up in the 1996 competition and were congratulated by the Judges for the overall quality of service offered.

Value your village shop - Use it don't lose it!

GARDEN COMPETITION RESULTS

MOST IMPROVED GARDEN	-	Mr. Cuthbert, 1 Badgers Walk
OMAR CHALLENGE CUP	-	Mrs. Robinson, 5 Oak Avenue
BEST SPRING GARDEN	-	Mrs. Brown, 19 Forest Way
BEST KEPT GARDEN AT DEANLAND	1st -	Miss Goode, 15 Badgers Walk
	2nd -	Mr. & Mrs. Willis, 3 Squirrel Drey
	3rd -	Mr. & Mrs. Ogden, 6 Sunset Avenue

MENTIONED IN DISPATCHES

Mr. & Mrs. Holland, 34 Badgers Walk
Mr. & Mrs. Beale, 1 Squrrel Drey
Mr. & Mrs. Russell, 2 Squirrel Drey
Mr. Green, 24 Woodpecker Lane
Mr. & Mrs. Pragnell, 5 Fox Hollow

* *

1996 - AND ALL THAT!

And so, another year is here
In fact, - well under way.
Such falling leaves we failed to clear
Have all been blown away,
Or lurk in nooks and crannies,
To appear another day.

The year that's gone was much the same
As all the ones before.
We reached the heights and plumbed the depths
As life composed its score.

Those New Year's resolutions made so determinedly
Have mostly faded from our minds,
- At least, if you're like me.

But, that is not important,
We know that in our hearts
We give up smoking, go on diets,
All in fits and starts.

The thing that really matters,
And stands above the rest,
Is that we try, as always,
To do our very best.

But - if that sounds a trifle prim,
Or maybe 'tongue in cheek',
I'll have to have another think.

Er - can you come back next week?

I LOVE SUMMER

Did you enjoy the Summer?
The lazy, hazy hours
Was ever sky a deeper blue?
Ever more brilliant flowers?

Did you notice how the pace of life
Slows in the sun's embrace?
A gentle stroll will reach your goal.
There is no need to race.

Did you have a little holiday?
Or simply stay at home.
Content with happy memories
Of sand and swirling foam.

Listening to the birds and bees;
Watching the squirrels in the trees.
Your limbs relaxed in summer ease;
Doing as you wish, and when you please

Watching the world go bustling by.
Such rush and tear is not for you.
You can rejoin it by and by
When dreamy summer days are through.

If so, then we're in tune, you see,
For that's what Summer means to me.
And, one more thing I'll say to you
- I really love the Autumn too
              - don't you?

CHRISTMAS

Oh, the jolly holly and the merry berry,
The wobbly jelly and the glittering tree.
The wonder of the wise men's journey;
　　The joy of the nativity.

The tinsel and the decorations.
The parties and the celebrations.
The greetings of friends and relations.
The planning and the preparation.
The cards, the presents, the embraces.
The happiness on children's faces.
The church bells, peeling, loud and clear.
Their message for us all to hear.

The comic mottos in the crackers.
The wondrous grottos in the stores.
The kisses 'neath the mistletoe.
The red, red robin in the snow.
The coloured fairy lights indoors.
The rich plum-pudding flamed in brandy.
The conversation to and fro.
The heavy laden festive table.
Jovial faces, all aglow.

The carol-singers with their story
Of the manger and its glory.
Surely no season's more sublime
Than happy, holy, Christmastime.

<u>Merry Christmas</u>

DEANLAND
'ASTORIA'
(Social Centre)

YOUR VERY OWN CINEMA

SPECIAL NOTICE   WE ARE AWARE THAT OUR FILM SHOWS HAVE BEEN 'DUBBED' "PEGGY AND RAY'S MICKEY MOUSE NITE" ——
AS WALT DISNEY PRODUCTIONS ARE SYNONYMOUS WITH TOP QUALITY, AND WE SHOW CLASSIC FILMS, WHICH MEANS - WORK OF RECOGNISED EXCELLENCE - IT THEREFORE APPEARS WE HAVE 'MADE IT ' TO THE TOP IN GOOD ENTERTAINMENT....

There's ALWAYS a VERY WARM WELCOME at the Deanland 'ASTORIA'.

DATE for YOUR calender :- WEDNESDAY 17th. SEPTEMBER 7-30 p.m.

We are proud to present

" P O C A H O N T A S "

A wonderful way to start our NEW SEASON of CLASSIC FILMS.......
An epic story of adventure - brought to life by breathtaking Disney animation, tells the story of courage and friendship, set against a backdrop of the New World - with delightful humour, powerful imagery and enchanting music. STUNNING COLOUR, STEREO SOUND.

It's a 'REEL' pleasure,
Peggy and Ray..

STOP PRESS. STOP PRESS. STOP PRESS. STOP PRESS. STOP PRESS.

WE ARE WORKING OURSELVES INTO A CELEBRATION - MAKE A DATE - WEDNESDAY 19th. NOVEMBER 7-30 p.m. Deanland 'ASTORIA' (Social Centre)

THE DEANLAND SINGERS

We hope you all enjoyed our Christmas Concert. I owe a big Thank You to George and the Singers for their efforts.

Your donations have enabled us to help launch a fund for the purchase of a "newer" organ for the Social Centre.

Looking forward to seeing you all at our Summer Concert.

Hilda Sanders

Music to the ears

* * * * * * *

WANTED

HAPPY NEW YEAR   1997

Consider, then – another year.
So swiftly time goes by.
Soon, now, the crocus will appear,
And winter wave 'goodbye'.

Last year was, well, much as the rest;
A mix of joy and pain.
Did your resolutions travel west?
Have you 'chanced your arm' again?

No matter how the years accrue,
Each January first
A fresh horizon comes in view,
And with it brings a thirst
To savour all the blessings
That each new season offers.
The treasure's there for all to share,
In nature's bounteous coffers.

Each bright new dawn on each new day
Provides a slate that's clear.
Gone are the doubts of yesterday;
They find no welcome here.

1997 is a book as yet unopened.
May every chapter, every page,
Be to your taste, my friend.

Happy New Year.

WELCOME BACK

It's here again . . .
The freshness and the newness.
The early morning dewness.
The skies of deeper blueness.
The whispered "I Love You"ness.

The dappled sunshine through the leaves.
The twittering nesting in the eaves.
The tingling stirrings of desire.
Rekindling of ambition's fire.

The glad acceptance, arms stretched wide,
Of all the season can provide.
The heady scent, and sight, and sound,
Of re-awakening all around.

Come look, come see, come hear it all,
The magic of sweet nature's call.
Burgeoning new life taking wing.
Rapturous, heart-warming, heavenly,

<u>Spring</u>.

SOMETHING ABOUT DEANLAND 1998

There's something about Deanland that
takes one unaware.
Can it be, I wonder, the friendliness that's there?

Or is it that the ready smile, of all you chance to meet
Promotes the sparkle to your eye;
the lightness to your feet?

Is it the proudly maintained homes that
nurtures ones content?
The beauty of the gardens;
the colours and the scent?

Is it the diet of peace and quiet that's there in
fullest measure?
Together with the boundless forms of leisure,
for your pleasure?

Whatever, of all these delights,
Deanland provides the lot.

Yes, there's something about Deanland.

It's a very pleasant spot!

ALL THE JOLLY

Is it really truly here again,
The frolic and the fun?
The mistletoe and fairylights
And gifts for everyone?

Those friends to whom you've meant to write,
The season of good cheer
Provides the perfect chance to let them know
 that you're still here.
A little card, it isn't hard, and yes, you'll
 surely, absolutely, be in touch with them
 next year.

Now, where's that list?
Who have I missed?
The hopes and expectations.
The stirring of shared memories
As you welcome your relations.
Oh, that this aura of goodwill could last
 throughout the year.
Perhaps it may, but for today let's thrust such
 pensiveness away,
For joy-bells ringing, carol-singing Christmas-time
 is here.

And then, as you sit, satisfied,
After your yuletime meal.
Relaxing for an hour or so
Before the 'high jinks' start.
Where are the words that could convey
The magic of this special day?
For sweet content is heaven sent,
With Christmas in your heart.

Happy Christmas

SPRING SONG　　　　　　　　　　　　　　　　1999

Oh, tra la la and fa la la.
Forget those cares and woes.
In Spring, the thing is to have a fling.
The season with the reason
To shed those winter clothes,
And say, 'Hey there, begone dull care,
It's Spring, so anything goes'.
When everything is fresh and new,
And leaden skies reclaim their blue.

When leaves are leafing, buds are budding.
Hopeful lovers' hearts are thudding.
Cattle lowing, farmers sowing.
Lambs are leaping, gardeners hoeing.
Holiday brochures on the table.
Shall we take our Auntie Mabel?
Everybody who is able,
Gird your loins and dance and sing
To the merry music of the Spring.

NEW SHOW HOME

YES its here at last! The new Sandringham Mark 3. It is based on the other two Sandringhams, one with a porch and the other with an ornamental exterior chimney.

As this Show Home is designed with the super view over our adjoining farmland, from plots on the new year 2000 'Meadows' development in mind, the front end has both a walk-in box bay window and full french doors leading out from the lounge into the garden.

I especially approve of the new utility room and the window seat in the guest bedroom.

Please come and look around, bring your friends and family.

P.S. As usual at Deanland, this special home already has future owners!

Tanya Head

IT'S A GIFT

The floral painting on my wall that lightened winter's gloom
Accepts that for a while it is redundant.
For naught can vie with all the splendour there outside my room,
And nature's glory everywhere abundant.
How lovingly the leaves have clothed the branches of each tree,
And how the birds strive to surpass each song.
Oh that this human frame of mine could for a fleeting hour
Fashion the grandeur of a tree, the beauty of a flower.
There is no way one could devise to match the magic of the skies,
The wonder of the dawn or setting sun.
And we should bend our knees in praise,
For we are blessed through all our days
That nature's gifts are there for everyone.

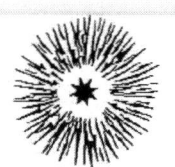

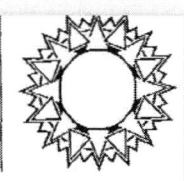

ECLIPSE OF THE SUN, August 11

Although there will be a total eclipse visible from southern Cornwall and southern Devon, only a partial eclipse will be visible from Deanland, where at maximum, about 11.22 a.m., 98% of the Sun will be obscured by the Moon: thus it will get noticeably darker around this time. The eclipse actually starts at 10.03 and ends at 12.41.

Don't look directly at the Sun at any time because of the risk of damage to your eyes. The eclipse can be seen safely by projecting an image of the Sun on to a white background, using a good pair of binoculars or a small telescope (this won't work with opera glasses)

There is a Solar Eclipse Party being held at Herstmonceux Science Centre in the morning. Advance bookings are required. I would recommend this option, particularly if you have grandchildren with you, since I'm sure that you will have the opportunity of viewing the eclipse safely, and also there will be hands-on activities for the children during the morning. This party is likely to be very much over-subscribed so if you fancy it, book immediately using the forms in the Deanland office.

Gordon E. Taylor

AUTUMN AVENUE.

Will you come with me for a little stroll
Down autumn avenue?
Where a gentle breeze stirs the drifting leaves,
And the sky's a steely blue.

Where the robin peers around as if
Seeking departed friends,
'Though one can tell he knows full well
The cooling climate sends
Them far away across the sea,
Whilst he stays here with you and me,
As if to make amends.

Where the field-mice search for shelter
Now the waist-high wheat is shorn,
And a silver sheen can be clearly seen
Glazing the grass each morn.

And the hedgerows gleam by the swelling stream
With berries white and red,
And all around upon the ground
The sun's pale light is shed.

Then, as we turn and head for home,
The cottage lamplights beckon.
That is my autumn avenue.
A pleasing one, I reckon.

CHRISTMAS 1999

Merrily the bells ring out their message of good cheer
It's the closing of the century, a very special year.
Let this yuletide prove to be a season of rebirth
Leading us, with hope, to our Nirvana - peace on earth.

Every loving greeting on every card we send
Not lasting just for Christmas, but for ever, without end.
Nobody excluded - no-one without a friend.
Icing on the Christmas cake, presents round the tree.
Underneath the mistletoe - a kiss or two or three ..(I wish!}

Merry Christmas everyone,
   and may we for the years to come
Walk hand-in-hand with happiness, in the millennium.

{In a period of 'style over content', the nation
was persuaded to overlook the fact that the
new millennium didn't begin until
1st January 2001
Ed.}

2000 - 2005

DEANLAND

DEC. / JAN. 2000

The Park entrance is a "hive of industry", with the Bowling Green well under way, and "The Meadows", our final phase of 23 homes, being pegged out and taking shape.

Our new hosts in the Tavern, Ian and Ivy, have made a good start, and we are hearing good reports of their efforts. So give the Tavern a try, particularly over the festive period.

Our shopkeepers, Terry and Eileen, also need your support, as our shop is vital to everyone on the Park, particularly as we all get older, and may not be able to get out as often to shop in these fancy big Supermarkets. They are doing their best, but report that not as many folk use the Shop as they would have expected.

That magical time, Christmas and the New Year are nearly with us. This time it is special with a new age dawning for the year 2000. To celebrate this unique, (in our lifetime) event, we are opening our "Millennium Walk". This is a purpose made and cleared track through our tree screen, and is accessed either at Badgers Walk at the Forest Way end, or Deer Haven by the log store, or Herons Way Exit Road by the refuse area. As soon as you see the signs go up, you can use it, but be careful, it is only a track through the woods. **PLEASE** make sure that your visiting children do not play in there alone. Always go with them if they want to use the "walk". Woodlands can be a dangerous place, and we will just have to close it if it is abused.

The other big event for the year 2000 celebrations is our Fete Weekend of **August 12 and 13**, it will probably take the form of an open weekend with our new Bowling Green, as well as the whole Park featuring in the event. More about this as we get closer to it. Please mark your diaries with the date, so as many folk can be around to show off their gardens and welcome visitors.

Finally for the New Years Eve, we are having a small fireworks display opposite Villa Content at midnight, all welcome to come and watch. Lets hope the weather lets us enjoy this special time.

A Very Happy Christmas and a Happy and Healthy New Year to all our readers
from Keith, Tanya and Nigel and all the staff at Deanland Wood Park

OPINION

GOINGS AND COMINGS.

I looked across the field, between the trees,
And fixed my eyes on
A figure I could just discern nearing the far horizon.
A trifle stooped, and walking slow, as if a little loath to go.
And, though the early-morning haze
Shrouded him somewhat from my gaze.
I saw him turn and wave, as in farewell.
And his voice, across the distance, held me as in a spell.

"<u>Think</u> of me, world," he said, - "and of all the years I've given.
Through triumph and disaster, from the birth of our religion.
From the wise men in the stable, to the brave men on the moon.
But, fear not, world, although my long sojourn with you is done
For, lo, - the new millennium is here."

And, sure enough, from out the trees I saw
A sprightly youth appear.
Oh. - He was good to look upon.
And, as they stood in fond embrace I heard the old man say,
"Good luck, son, with the human race, I must be on my way."
And the young man spoke with verve and zest.
His voice, clear as a bell.
"My friend, go confidently to rest.
I have my orders from above,
To lead the world in peace and love.
And, verily, I'll serve our master well."

It must have been imagination made these visions come to me.
Yet they bequeathed sweet anticipation for the 21st century.

INTO SPRING

As a graceful ballerina
Has the power to entrance.
Pirouette and entrechat
Holding you, whoe'er you are,
With the beauty of her dance.

So does springtime claim our senses,
Gently nudging our defences
With the charm of its advance.

Fragrance clings to gentle breezes.
Daffodils sway in proud delight.
Nature graciously releases
All her wonders to our sight.

Magic mantles all the seasons
With the glamour that they bring,
And for, oh, so many reasons,
Who can but <u>adore</u> the spring.

SUMMER'S HERE

Summer's here, - Tra-La.
Let's give it a greeting.
Sapphire skies and strawberries.
Free gratis solar heating.

Dappled leafy lanes with cosy dry-bank seating.
Twittering birds and murmuring streams,
Purpose-fashioned, so it seems,
For happy lovers meeting.

Deckchairs on the lawn
To while away the hours.
Roses rambling on the fence.
All around the heady scents
Of brilliant summer flowers.

Happy, hazy, lazy days.
Would they'd not pass so soon.
Still, - Let us sing a song of praise.
For it is <u>only</u> June. -- Hurrah!

INTO AUTUMN

The mantle of the evening gathers softly as a sigh.
Imperceptibly increasing as the shortening days go by.
The laden branches quiver as they brace to shed their leaves,
And the birds that stay seek sanctuary beneath the
  beckoning eaves.

The sky has a metallic hue as grey impinges on the blue,
And thickening cloud-banks group and grow and, heavy-laden,
  hover low.
And all around and everywhere there is a keenness in the air.

And if one listens for a spell with heart and soul and reason
The breeze is whispering 'farewell' to the sleepy, sated
Summer season.
And listen more because 'tis sure 'twill be sweet music to
  the ears.
As autumn sings 'I'm here, I'm here', and in radiant russet
  robe appears.

David Bellamy Conservation Awards

I am pleased to announce that we have been awarded a **GOLD** in our recent application. Thank you to all who responded with the postcards. The judges were particularly impressed with our new Woodland Walk.

CAN IT BE?

Can it be that time again when Christmas bells are ringing?
When Santa's loading up his sleigh and rallying Rudolph
from the hay, and carollers are singing?

When shops are stocked with festive cheer and pubs are
Crammed with extra beer.
When mother's busy as can be and father's fussing
with the tree.
When card and gift lists pile so high one wonders should one
laugh or cry.
When children are as good as gold. -- 'Please hurry, Mum,
-- before it's sold.'

When snow lies deep on the window-cill and all around seems
hushed and still.
When the amber moon seems just shoulder-high in the
midnight-blue of the star-strewn sky.
When there's a dampness to the eye as heightened recollections
fly to tender Christmases gone by.
When the very air is filled with greetings and plans are made
for Yuletide meetings.

When lips curve upwards in a smile as humdrum cares are
shelved awhile.
When cakes are iced and trees are lit and love and laughter's
the heart of it.
Can it be that it's nearly here; the Holy Birthday we revere?
Well, -- it is on its way, -- oh, yes!
May the gift it brings be happiness.

Merry Christmas

DEANLAND

DEC/JAN 2001

Can you believe all this water, where has it all come from? The 12 October 2000, when Lewes and Uckfield flooded will go down in history as a natural disaster! But it kept on raining on and off for nearly a month. The ground became waterlogged, and large areas of the north, flooded and lost power for days.

We are so lucky here at Deanland Park, that through all these extreme problems, the Park only had flooding in its sewer system. This was caused by all the pipes and settlement tanks being underground, as they are usually, and the water level in the ground being just at the surface level. Water then tries to fill the pipes and tanks under pressure from the ground, they usually succeed, and we have to set up extra pumps to help control it. This all generally happens in the middle of the night, and this time was no exception. The good news is that we managed to maintain control over all our sewers during this worrying period. However we must all bear in mind that this is an exceptional period of heavy rain, and the water level in the ground is just under the surface. Therefore you must expect puddles in your gardens with areas of water laying for longer than normal, but it will all go away in time.

One good thing has come from all this wind and rain and that is the leaves and acorns seem to have all come down at once. Acorns are a problem this time of the year and in the New Forest they used to allow pig farmers to graze the forest with their pigs, who feed on acorns. I thought about doing that here, but could not imagine the effect of lots of pigs running loose around the Park. But it would get rid of the acorns! Before you start putting pen to paper, I am joking!

I am working on a Website for the Park, and have reserved www.deanlandpark.com as the address, it should be available very soon. Please have a look and tell your friends if you like it, or let me know if you do not.

It is election time coming up next May for the County Council and maybe a General Election, anyone needing a postal vote please let me know. This will apply if you are going to be away or on holiday during May 2001.

As you know the Tavern is now closed for refurbishment, and the plans have been finalised, more about this further on.

The festive season is just round the corner, lets hope that the really bad weather is now behind us, and we can enjoy this lovely part of England.

A very Happy Christmas and a healthy and peaceful New Year to all our readers

Keith Whitehead

OPINION

SUCH A THING

2001

The air is sparkling, clear and fine.
Tingling the lips like new-chilled wine.
Roofs shine in glistening silhouette
Where morning dew lies icy yet.
Temptation is a fireside-chair,
 - - When winter's there.

Frost-silvered branches bend and sigh,
Outlined against the sombre sky.
And underfoot the brittle ground
Bequeaths each step a crunching sound.
And the curlew's plaintive call is clear,
 - - When winter's here.

And, through the yet-reluctant earth,
A tiny flower seeks rebirth.
Blossoming there for our delight.
A welcome and heart-warming sight.
Oh, - such an optimistic thing;
The crocus, - - harbinger of spring.

The Tavern

So what's happening? The main point is, that the Tavern is remaining the same, i.e., a smaller Bar and a Function Room in the same places as they are now. I have decided not to move our office into the building. There will be the ability to fold back partitions to make one large room. Both Bars will be removed and replaced with one Bar that can serve both rooms without the staff leaving the Bar area. All the unused areas of the old children's room, and other lobbies will be brought into use as part of the two main rooms. New entrances will be formed, and two large fanlight openings will be made in the ceiling to let light in. The toilets will be re-built in their present position, the "old" office on the side will become a Bowls Clubroom and rented to the Bowls Club. Next to that, will be added a disabled toilet facility, accessible by the Tavern and the Bowls Club. Smoke treatment filters will be fitted and "no smoking" areas allocated. The windows will all be replaced, a new central heating system and the kitchen refitted and modernised. All future functions will have to be linked to the Park or a member of the Park, to avoid unnecessary noise either from the building, or from the car park.

Work should commence before Christmas and the search for a new tenant will begin in earnest in the new year, with a view to opening around Spring 2001

We may change the name, any ideas? Please let me know, and I will give a bottle of whisky or similar to the person who supplies a name that we decide to use.

'ASTORIA'
(Social Centre)

YOUR VERY OWN CINEMA

Dates for your calendar - 21st February at 7.30pm
"Could we see it again?" film - we are proudly showing this month:-

THE JOLSON STORY

Songs galore that will live forever sung by Al Jolson the one and only - Larry Parks playing the lead - this is first class entertainment, a movie to really brighten up a February evening.

21st March at 7.30pm
A film presentation TOO BIG for our screen - but we'll cope

BEN HUR

The only film to win 11 Oscars!! The most honoured film comes to Deanland 'Astoria' on this March evening, starring Charlton Heston, Stephen Boyd, Jack Hawkins, Haya Harareet, Hugh Griffith, Martha Scott, Sam Jaffe and Finlay Currie.
A story of one man's struggle against the might of the Roman Empire - magnificent action in the sea battle and the chariot race will never be forgotten!!

A 'reel' pleasure
Ray Young

* * * * * * * * * * * * * * * * * * *

THE ORGAN CLUB ENTERTAINERS

We are presenting a programme of music and frivolity on Sunday 11th March at 2.00pm and 7.30pm.

Our Organ Club Fundraising during the past few months amounted to £867.00 and with a donation from the Social Club, has enabled us to purchase a brand new electric piano for £1,028.00. (Our thanks to Peter Drage who bargained with Bonners Music, and got the price reduced from £1,299.00).

This piano and the organ that we purchased last year for the Social Centre, will all help to make our Concerts a great success. Our special thanks to Robin Bratton, for all his fundraising.

Proceeds from a collection will be given to The Deanland Day Centre.

We hope you will all enjoy our efforts.

Emily Bright.

IT'S NICE

It's nice:
To see the burgeoning trees,
   Bejewelled with blossom pink and white.
   Daffodils dancing in the breeze,
   And yellow-gold forsythia.

To hear the birds sing sweet and clear
   In all increasing rapture,
   So happy they the time in here,
   And everything awakening.

To sit beside a sparkling stream,
   On fragrant moss-clad banks,
   'Neath fluffy clouds, 'midst meadows green,
   And distant cattle grazing.

No need is there to 'phone a friend or wonder why
   or anything.
It's nice because it's SPRING!

DEANLAND SINGERS

INVITE **YOU** TO OUR

OLD TYME CONCERT

ON SATURDAY 18th. AUGUST AT 2.30 p.m.

AND SUNDAY 19th. AUGUST AT 7.30 p.m.

WHY NOT JOIN IN THE FUN AND WEAR

VICTORIAN/EDWARDIAN CLOTHES!!!

DAME VERA LYNN D.B.E, LL.D.

Hampton Cryst
Common Lane
Ditchling
Sussex
BN6 8TS

Dear Deanland Singers,

Thank you so much for the cheque £10 for the "School for Parents". Will you also thank Mr & Mrs Hickmott. You may like to know that we have now raised enough to carry us through the next year. We must still work hard to make sure the school continues for years ahead.

Please give my respects to all the residents, and hope they are not too depressed at this weather. Never mind! Spring is coming! The sooner, we hope.

Yours
Vera Lynn

The Deanland Singers have donated £150.00 to Dame Vera Lynn's charity S.O.S. We received this letter from Dame Vera.

NOT ONLY

It isn't just the holly and the mistletoe.
The cards and all the presents round the tree,
The robin hopping merrily across the sparkling snow
The jovial, smiling faces that you see.

It isn't just the carollers
Thronging round the door,
The sound of church-bells on the frosty air.
It isn't even all the laughs
The singing and the jokes,
The happiness of Christmas that you share.

It isn't just that all these things
Don't play their special part.
But the wonder that this season brings,
The sense of holiness that clings,
Lies deep within your heart.

Happy Christmas

HURRAH FOR SPRING   2002

Winter seems reluctant to relinquish its domain,

And leaves behind a legacy of winds and driving rain,
As if to say-- remember me till I come back again.

Whilst spring, there on the sidelines, waiting calmly
First in queue,
Mixes in her palette a brighter shade of blue.
She paints the sky and then selects a lovely emerald green,
And spreads it like a carpet where the frost has lately been.
She marshals all the songbirds and
Reminds them of their score.
Then settles to the task of coaxing seedlings through
Once more.
And, like a lady bountiful out upon a spree, she scatters
Flowers of every hue far as the eye can see.
She clothes each tree with green and gold and mauve and
Pink and white,
And there is no mistake the extent of her delight.

And who would not be proud, one asks, to conjure every year
An ambience that so enchants the eye, the mind, the ear.
That lifts the heart and bolsters hope and lightens everything.
And makes the young seek for a mate and the old conject it's
Not too late, perhaps, for one more fling.

Oh, yes indeed -- Hurrah for Spring.

THE MOON IN JUNE

When I was young, the moon in June was all
That I could ask.
With the one I loved beside me, in its radiance
We would bask.
The gentle rustle of the trees as we sat beside
The stream
And whispered of future that would outshine
Any dream.
The scent across the meadow from the slowly-ripening
Corn.
In June, love's tune can make you feel so lucky
You were born.
Now that I'm old the moon in June, of course, is
Still about.
Even my failing eyesight tells me that.
But the tune it sings is different; somehow it's
Lost its clout.
Or maybe it's that I no longer know just what
I'm at.
But, when I come to think of it, all that stuff
About the stream, and waving corn and such is
Quite untrue.
For when I was young, I sometimes couldn't even see
The moon.
The lowering factory chimneys blocked my view.
It might at times reflect back from the top-deck of
A tram.
   .. 'Cos a proper bloomin' Cockney's what I am.
   - - - - - - - - - - - - - -
(Still, . . . it's the stuff that dreams are made of).

NOT LATELY

They used to walk with feathered tread.
<u>Now</u>, though, they walk sedately.
Once laughed aloud, - now <u>smile</u> instead.
- - - He hasn't kissed her lately.

Once he acclaimed her golden curls.
Said he admired them greatly.
Deemed her above all other girls.
- - - He hasn't kissed her lately.

The years have flown, as is their way,
But should you ask her, she would say
She doesn't really mind the grey.
- - - He hasn't kissed her lately.

I beg you, don't be led astray
And deem the man's love fickle.
There's lots of hugging every day
And loads of 'slap-and-tickle'.

He hasn't kissed her lately for,
In all life's hurly-burly,
<u>Some</u> things cannot be waited for.
- - - So they kiss each morning, - - early.

THE ART GROUP

Yes - we are still operational!

And we would be pleased to welcome all the nice people who tell us they want to come along - but where are you all!

Incidentally our 'SUMMER EXHIBITION' this year will be held on Sunday 12th August, the day after the Deanland Fete, in the Social Centre from 10.00am to 4.00pm. Free admission. Everyone welcome!

AS THE CASE MAY BE.

As I'm sitting in my sun-room.
My favourite 'when-work-is-done' room;
Or even <u>'not-done'</u>, - as the case may be.
I look out upon a vista that is pleasing to the eye.
Fields nudging the horizon and trees reaching for the sky.

And it is quiet and serene, and lets my thoughts aspire,
As I look into the graceful branches climbing higher and higher,
Of years ago, when I was young,
Before a blazing hearth and conjuring pictures in the fire.

And, today, between the leafy spaces,
I can see houses, ships and faces,
Shimmering and changing at the whimsy of the breeze.
And they evoke lost memories and foster new desires,
In imagination's scenery of minarets and spires.

And it's a <u>harmless</u> pastime, as I'm sure you will agree,
Finding dreams and inspiration in the branches of a tree.
And; when my conscience stirs me; - as it sometimes does, of course.
Despite this silly story, may I ask <u>please</u> don't ignore me
Should we chance to meet outdoors.

For I promise not to mention
What I picture in a tree,
When the chores are done, - or <u>not</u> done;
<u>Just</u> as the case may be.

DEANLAND

OCT/NOV 2001

Nothing reinforces more the tranquillity and beauty of **Deanland Park** than the terrible events in New York on the 11 September. I still cannot come to terms with the massive loss of life. The terrorist total disregard for their life is also difficult to comprehend. It questions the whole basis of our existence, which is based upon the need to live and survive. The world, I fear will never be the same again. Our hearts go out to everyone, whatever nationality that lost friends and loved ones in this awful event.

The **Inn on The Park** has opened with a very successful two days, that saw nearly everyone living here coming to have a look. I can speak from experience the food is great!! Roy & Linda have made a good start and are now up to strength with staff. We welcome the chef, Michael, as well as Pam and Chris who are "front of house", together with all the family and friends of Roy & Linda who regularly help out in the "pub". By the way, anyone interested in a cleaning job in the new "pub", contact Roy or Linda on 872406

In Memory of Emily Bright

Ron would like to let you know that a total of £316.00 has been raised and donated to Macmillan Cancer Relief, Eastbourne & Country Healthcare Palliative Care Fund and Children in Need. These wonderful sums of money have been donated from friends on the Park, and other friends and family of Emily and Ron. This money has been acknowledged from the various benefactors.

Ron has asked to express here his grateful thanks to Rev. David Farey for the care and kind words he put into Emily's funeral service, which were gratefully appreciated by him and his family.

OUR EMILY

In the very many years I've spent upon this earth
I've learned to test the value of what true friendship's worth.
And to know someone like Emily has been a pride and joy,
And leaves me with a memory that nothing can destroy.

Her gentle sense of humour,
Her all-embracing smile.
The kindliness in all she said
Made everything worthwhile.

And, when we hear an organ played,
Or when the singing starts,
Our Emily will still be with us,
Deep within our hearts.

When Emily sang, the song she chose seemed to become her own.
And her gentle touch on the organ-keys was surely hers alone.
Her love for Ron and family seemed heavenly inspired.
And one feels, with them and Deanland, Em had all her heart desired.
And there is nothing surer, without Emily Deanland's much the poorer.
And may I voice for all of us this message which is true,
- You'll always be our Emily.
- Thanks, Em, for being you.

Doris

MORE ABOUT EMILY

If you will kindly bear with me,

I'll take this opportunity
To talk about a woman whom
To <u>know</u> was to admire.

There are, of course a lot of those;
'Tis a bonus of our sex.
But, sometimes, in life's ebbs and flows
One comes across a special gem,
We did just <u>that</u>, her name was Em.

And as a gem we treasured her,
And held her in esteem.
To put it in another way
Perhaps the best thing I can say
Is, if Deanland were a cup of coffee.
Then Em was the <u>cream</u>.

She was the sort who seemed to add
Lustre to every day.
From the time that I first knew her
It always seemed that way.

Should one want to share a laugh.
Em was the one to find.
And, if in need of sympathy
No-one could be more kind.

We loved her music, loved her songs.
Loved having her around.
Emily was surely someone whose
Like is rarely found.

Cont...

And, though no longer part of
Our daily Deanland scene,
Emily's there right at the heart of
Where she has always been.
And I can't find a finer way
To register Emily's praise
Than to sing her songs and think of her
Each time an organ plays.

> **CAROLS ON THE PARK**
> (weather permitting)
>
> It does not seem possible, that a year has passed since the last "Carols on the Park".
> We will once again be bringing Santa and his helpers to entertain you
>
> **Tuesday 17th December, commencing 7.00pm**
>
> All procceds will be given to support the very worthwhile work of the Macmillan nurses.
>
> Listen for a tin rattling near you!!
>
> *Eileen Ledger*

TO 2003

Let us, in 2003, have heart and head held high.
And hope in the ascendancy now the old year's waved goodbye.
No-one can tell what lies ahead; what the New Year has in store.
But, gold or dross; be it gain or loss we've known it all before.

So let us concentrate each day on the wonders everywhere.
The myriad marvels of the world there for us all to share.
Life's an adventure all the way, so make the most of every day.
Live to the full and you will see how great 2003 can be.

HAILSHAM FARMERS' PRODUCE & CRAFT MARKET

Hailsham Cattle Market, Market Street
from 9am to 1pm

2ND SATURDAY EVERY MONTH FOR 2003

January	11th	July	12th
February	8th	August	9th
March	8th	September	13th
April	12th	October	11th
May	10th	November	8th
June	14th	December	13th

Fresh local produce to include a variety of organic goods.
Vegetables - fruit - meat - eggs - bread - cakes
plants - honey - pickles - dairy products -
and our unique Crafts section . . .

MARKET CAFE

Further details contact Janet Du...

Supported by Wealden...

DEANLAND spring

Spring Fayre and Craft Show
This will take place on Saturday May 3rd at 10.30am in the hall.

Nearly New stall – please take any items for sale to the side door by the garages at 9.15am on the morning of the Fayre.

Cake stall – cakes, preserves, biscuits etc, home made or bought will be welcomed for sale.

Lastly please come along and support us on the day all are welcomed

Jackie Carter
Secretary.

PARK NEWS - SOCIAL CLUB

DEANLAND ASTORIA
(Your very own Cinema in the Social Centre)

Wednesday 16th April at 7.30pm

To end the season a great film
OLIVER

Six Oscar Awards need I say more?

Hope you have enjoyed the presentations.
Thank you for your support
Roy Young

A SPRINGTIME STROLL

Oh, come with me and greet the spring.
We'll maybe find a fairy ring.
Perchance espy the fairy queen,
In gossamer gown of gold and green
And, possibly, from 'neath the earth
We'll hear the murmurs of rebirth
As nature waves her magic wand
And every meadow, tree and pond
Awake in answer to her voice.
And we will, you and I, rejoice
As though the dewy grass we roam
Back to the haven of our home,
With sparkling memories that cling.
Such are the splendours of the spring.

MEMORY LANE

I took a trip down memory lane
To see what I could find.
I took no luggage with me;
Only an open mind.

I didn't need a bus or train,
Nor yet a car or aeroplane.
No need for them to take the strain.
I just let instinct guide my brain,
   - and there I was, - a child again.

And oh, the joy, and oh, the pleasure
There is in looking back.
The things one thought were lost for ever
Are there again, on track.

I looked round this wonderland I'd found
And spied an empty sack.
I thought that I would gather up
The memories one by one,
And fetch them back across the years
When this wondrous trip was done.
Then I would have them close at hand
When I was back in adult-land.

And soon the sack was overflowing
And I told myself I must be going.
So I waved goodbye to all my friends,
And told them, "Have no fear"
I pointed to the sack and said,
"This isn't where your story ends.
I've got you safe in here".

And, later on, when I awoke,
Amongst familiar things,
It took a little while to break
The fantasy a day-dream brings.

In fact, I took a hasty glance,
In case the sack was there perchance.
Then smiled to myself and said,
"Of course it's still there in my head,
And I'll find all my friends again
On my next trip down memory lane."

IN PRAISE OF - - -

It's nice to live at Deanland,

With all Its grass and treeses.
Where friendly folk say 'bless you',
Whenever someone sneezes.

It's great at the social centre,
Where we play our games-ee-waymses.
And, should one's skill be good or ill,
There are no moans or blameses.

It's fine at the shopsy-wopsy,
Where the stock meets all our needses.
And the pleasant smiles and special offers
Are easy on our minds and coffers.

Not to mention the pubsy-wubsy,
Where, besides all the drinksy-winksy,
And entertainment to divert,
There's plenty of lovely grubsy.

Even more than these thingsy-wingsies,
There's our very own bussy-wussy,
And bowling-green, and swimming-pool.
Oh, - lucky-wussy ussy!

So, - here's to good old Deanland,
With all its grass and treeses.
Where folk are nice and friendly,
- and where every prospect pleases.

--- Now, should this rhymesy-wymesy
Make you think I'm past my timesy.
Look at it as another way of saying what I want
To say,
--- and -- it <u>isn't</u> any <u>crimesy</u>. --- <u>See</u>?

THE FLOWER OF FRIENDSHIP

So many lovely flowers grace a garden,
Imbuing joy and solace to the eye.
And how divinely the perfume
Wafting from a fragile bloom
Bequeaths a new dimension
to the azure summer sky.

Yes, there are wondrous flowers in a garden,
Yet, even so, there's one that stands apart.
A precious bloom that always stays,
Through every season, all your days,

And dwells within the precincts of your heart.
No earthly storm or hurricane can bend it.
Life's slings and arrows firm its roots more true.
It is the transcendental flower of friendship.
May it flourish everlastingly for you.

Thanks

A big thank you to all the hardworking deliverers of the Deanland News over the past year, we are extremely grateful, as I know all the folk who receive it are.

We should also like to thank the ladies who look after the Doctors Surgery for the time they give up free of charge to make your visit to the surgery pleasant and comfortable.

2004

Well, - here we are, as we've been before.
-- Now it's the year two thousand and four.
A pristine canvas on which to draw.
How many plus marks will we score?

Will we attain top of the board?
And will our dreams bear fruit?
Or will the New Year plans we've made
Be pruned, our moods to suit?

Will the graph of life go up or down?
Which shall prevail, - the laugh or frown?
Oh, please let laughter gain the crown.

And, if apathy tries to sidle in,
<u>Don't</u> proffer it an easy win.
Try, try again, and then some more.
<u>And have a great two thousand and four.</u>

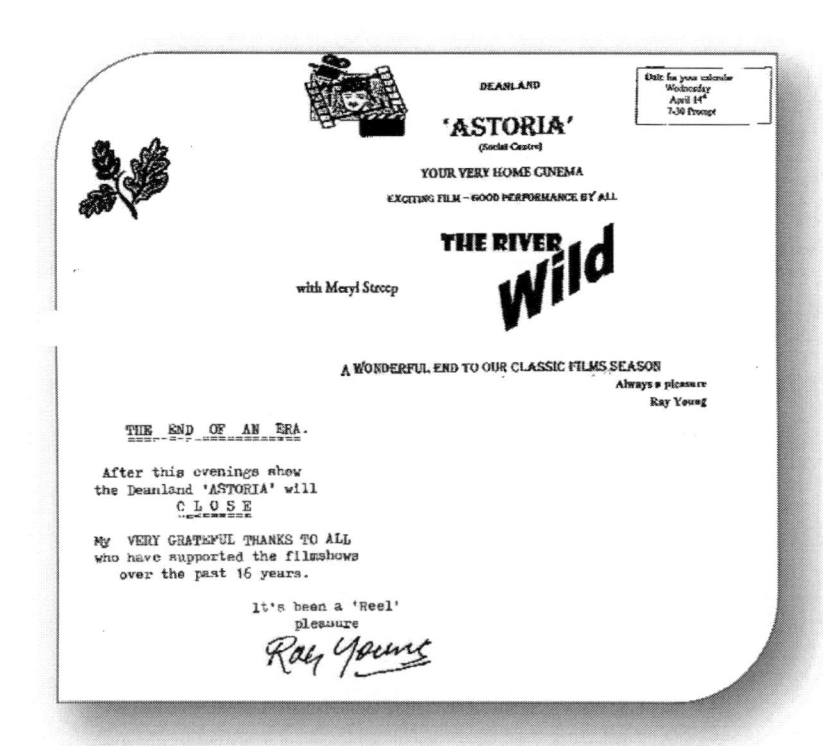

DEANLAND

'ASTORIA'
(Social Centre)

YOUR VERY HOME CINEMA

EXCITING FILM – GOOD PERFORMANCE BY ALL

THE RIVER wild

with Meryl Streep

Date for your calendar
Wednesday
April 14th
7.30 Prompt

A WONDERFUL END TO OUR CLASSIC FILMS SEASON

Always a pleasure
Ray Young

THE END OF AN ERA.

After this evenings show
the Deanland 'ASTORIA' will
C L O S E

My VERY GRATEFUL THANKS TO ALL
who have supported the filmshows
over the past 16 years.

It's been a 'Reel'
pleasure

Ray Young

SOMETHING ABOUT SPRING

The spring! -- Earth's re-awakening.
When nature casts aside her winter shawl,
And starts to sort the 'goodies' for us all.
When gardeners no longer lie abed,
But, full of plans, approach the potting-shed.

When windows are thrown wide
To let the scented air inside,
And minds clock-on to 'impulse-shopping',
Now that heating costs are dropping.

And the crocus and forsythia appear in all their glory.
And fledglings break out from their shells
To sing the springtime story.

And the lambs leap in the meadows,
And, - their shyness gone away,
Tongue-tied youths do suddenly find quite a lot to say.

And old folk reminisce about the bliss of
Their first kiss,
And seedlings struggle through the soil to
Seek the light of day.
And the trees shake off their lethargy, to
Show how green their leaves can be.

And, no matter at what stage you are.
Begone dull care what age you are.
You feel you're fit for <u>anything</u>.
--- <u>Such</u> are the splendours of the Spring.

END OF A PERFECT DAY

When the sun is sinking in the west and the moon is standing by.
When the stars collect their twinkles and disperse across the sky.
When the final sleepy starling reaches his cosy nest.
When the little ones are all abed and the labourer at rest.
When the bedtime story has been told and the lullaby been sung,
And the blessed sleep of innocence lays claim upon the young.
When the business of the day is done and the late-night shopping finished.
The last bus is in the depot and the traffic is diminished.
When the evening-meal is over and the dishes washed and dried.
And the rain is slamming on the roof whilst all is snug inside.
When you know that for some hours at least you can relax at leisure,
The sense of satisfaction in your heart is beyond measure.
For there's nothing so rewarding as the close of a lovely day,
When everything has turned out well and plans have gone your way.
And this is what I wish for you; freedom from strife or sorrow.
May every day be pleasing,
              - and improve with each tomorrow.

LOOKING BACK

I'm at an age where my allotted span
Is so far back it's an 'also-ran'.
An age where one can ponder at
The goings-on of this and that.
An age where childhood memories
Are like a page in history.
But, even though they are long gone,
As with history, times and facts live on.

And why? I ask you, - should they not?
<u>Why</u> should such memories be forgot?
                - (poetic license.)
Each life is its own history book.
Each has its tale to tell.
And, though to others it may seem of
Small account,
<u>You</u> reign supreme. <u>Yours</u> is the dream.
<u>Your</u> reminiscences amount to the world
In which you dwell.

So, close your mind to the white hair;
Ignore the double-chin.
What if your 'get-up-and-go' has gone.
<u>Enjoy</u> the skin you're in.

Revel in dreams of yesteryear:
When love was new and all was fun.
Remember, though, that whilst still here
Your personal saga isn't done.

So, make the most of every day.
<u>Enjoy</u> each passing minute.
God writes the final history book;
-- And <u>your</u> page will be in it.

DEANLAND ART GROUP

To let you all know, the date of our 'pre' Christmas Exhibition this year will be Sunday 28th November 10.00am – 4.00pm
Our standard of work is still high, and should be well worth a visit!
"FEEL FREE TO COME BROWSE"

Deanland Singers

The Deanland Singers wish to thank all our friends who gave so generously at our Concerts. We now have an amount of £300.00 to give towards a worthwhile project. This amount covers the Concerts given in 2003 and our Summer Concert this year.

On this occasion we will be giving the donation to Eastbourne Hospital. Most of us 'Old 'Uns' have received care and attention from our local hospital and I am sure they will be able to put such substantial sum to good use. In the event it is used for a specific purpose we will let you know in due course.

Thank you all once again for your generosity.

A PLEASANT OUTING

There's a little place I know,
<u>Not</u> very far from here,
That really sets my heart aglow
And fills me with good cheer.

It's down the lane a little way,
Then up a gentle hill.
Round a couple of easy corners.
You can <u>come</u> there if you will.

And we could share the charm of it;
And I am very sure
You'll like it, just as much as <u>me</u>.
You <u>couldn't</u> like it <u>more</u>.

There'd be no need to hurry.
We <u>wouldn't</u> have to worry.
And it would be so wonderful
To wander and explore.

With the map of life to guide us
No misfortune could betide us.
It would be like a <u>holiday</u> I guess.

You'll find it in no time at all.
It's name is written on the wall.
Don't think I <u>need</u> to tell you.
-- They <u>call</u> it 'Happiness'.

A "BIT OF A DO" IS DONE

We've done it - we've done it - we've done it.
We've pulled off· 'A Bit of a Do.'
Went in for the test, and we've won it.
All of us. You -You and You.

We ventured outside our home circuit.
With hearts in our mouths - at least mine,
Not knowing for sure if we'd work it,
Or end up with the dread 'thumbs down' sign.

But - no; it went over with 'bells on'.
Our efforts had not been in vain.
And left us with memories to dwell on.
And the thought - p'raps we'll do it again.

But. whether we do or we do not.
This memory will live with us long.
For when put to the test we all gave of our best.
And to try hard can never be wrong.

So, here's to Deanland Entertainers.
And, here's to ·'A Bit of a Do'.
It was great - It was fun.
We tried and we won.
And, I'm happy about that ...... Aren't you?

DEANLAND ENTERTAINERS

The Deanland Entertainers ventured to pastures new, to put on their show "A Bit Of A Do" in front of an audience of a 100 plus, at the Charles Hunt Centre in Hailsham, on Friday 27th August 2004

FESTIVE FANCIES

Hey, - it's Christmas-time again.
Season of fun and laughter.
When you 'butter-up' the ones you love,
To get that thing you're after.

Oh, - I don't really <u>mean</u> it,
For that is just <u>not</u> you.
The ones you love, you <u>really</u> love,
- The <u>whole</u> time; all year through.

Are the Christmas cards all written?
The presents wrapped and hidden?
If they <u>are</u>, it's <u>you</u> who should be
The star a'top the Christmas tree.

But, it will all get done in time,
The way it always has.
And then you'll hear the church-bells chime,
And enjoy the razzmatazz.

And, when you break the wishbone,
May the large bit come to you.
And may you 'Go to Town' on it,
And your wishes all come true.

- - - Happy Christmas.

CAROLS AROUND THE PARK

A date for your diaries – Tuesday 14ᵗʰ December

We will again be coming around the park Singing Carols and collecting for Macmillan Cancer Research.

Anyone wishing to take part please meet in the car park,
ready to set off at 7:00pm

We collected just over £400 last year, so let's see if we can beat that this year!

Any further information – please phone me on
Barbara Roberts

DEANLAND News

Dec94/Jan95

50 Years

- INFORMATION DESK
- SOCIAL CALENDAR
- PARK NEWS
- DEANLAND ESTATES

DEANLAND PARK HOMES
PARK HOMES ESTATE
www.deanlandpark.co.uk

2000 DAVID BELLAMY CONSERVATION AWARD GOLD

DEANLAND

DEC / JAN 2005

As this 50th Anniversary year slowly comes to an end, we have had plenty of time to reflect on the past times, both good and bad. In those early days of the 50's when there was no mains water or sewage and a very weak electricity system, to today's modern Park with all the mains services including natural gas. Sewage is not strictly "mains" as we have five treatment works throughout the Park. Over the years we have been through the heavy snows of the winter of 1963, the "hurricane" of 1987, wet winters, dry summers, all human life is here! Long may it continue I hear you say! The celebrations of this 50th anniversary are now drawing to an end; we have enjoyed our celebration dinner at the Inn on the Park in October. Our thanks go to the staff of the "pub" for making the evening memorable. It just shows you what can be produced at the "pub" and what a great time can be had. Profits in the drug company "Alka Seltzer" went up hugely the following day, I wonder why?

It is not over yet, everyone who lives on the Park, is invited to join us and our families for mulled wine and a mince pie on the run up to Christmas at the Inn on the Park. The dates and times are: Monday 13 December and Wednesday 15 December. More details further on. We look forward to some Christmas cheer to finish this happy occasion of our 50th Anniversary.

This year also saw the retirement of Florrie Wilsher, as Chairman of the Social Centre committee. I cannot let her standing down as committee Chairman go by without paying tribute to the enormous amount of work and dedication she brought to the Social Centre over the 16 years or so, that she presided over the committee. Our grateful thanks go to Florrie for all she has done and we wish her a happy retirement at sunny Deanland Park.

The **Deanland Bus** has given us good service for the last 13 years or so, but it is due for replacement and as I said in a previous Deanland News, that we would not replace it, but keep it going as long as we have driver and the bus does not become too expensive to run. Well, it has become too expensive to run, as it now runs at a loss, also our excellent driver Rod McFarlane, has indicated that he wishes to give up. It is interesting to note, that when the bus first started running a regular timetable to Hailsham and Eastbourne, way back in 1991, there was very little, if any at all, regular service picking up at the Park. Now we have at least three service buses calling in and returning to the Park. This includes the Cuckmere Community Bus, which is similar in size to our bus. The Cuckmere Community Bus will increase their service to the Park to fill the gaps that are left when our bus stops. More details further on. I should like to thank Rod for the cheerful way he has carried out his tasks as driver and all the help he has given to all the folk on the Park in the time he has been "in charge" of the bus.

The Deanland Bus will finish at Christmas and the Cuckmere Community Bus will commence its new timetable on the 5th January 2005.

We, the family owners of the Park and all our staff wish you all a very

MERRY CHRISTMAS AND A HAPPY NEW YEAR

Keith Whitehead

PARK NEWS

TO 2005

Now the Christmas lights are taken down,
The garlands put away,
We leave them with our memories,
To live another day.
2004 is over, with its mix of joy and sorrow,
And another untouched year is here;
    ---   A new tomorrow.

Another year; another chance
To give our latent plans a glance.
Fresh opportunity to start
Those ventures closest to our heart.
Those resolutions dropped last year,
The chance to pick them up is here.

That's if you're still of the same mind,
For our requirements change, I find,
And our desires are fickle.
So the urge that was an itch last year
May now be just a tickle.

Just make the most of every day.
Each dawn is a new start,
And the sun will shift the darkest clouds
Whilst there's hope within your heart.

And as the days go drifting by
With their duties and their leisure,
May happiness warm each hearth and home,
And peace in fullest measure.

May friends be true, and may we have the best of
Health, and thrive,
    ---   In 2005.

HERE AGAIN

Somebody's opened up the door and winter's
Filtered out.
Lighter mornings; brighter days, -
What is it all about?

The answer is whispered in the breeze,
And through the branches of the trees.
Such a thing! -- It's <u>Spring</u>.

What a joy, what a pleasure,
As the season spreads its treasure.
Daffodils to greet the sun.
Lighter hearts for everyone.

Seedlings thrusting through the earth
Struggling for all they're worth
To gain a hold in their domain
And blossom sweet and fair again.

Iron out those frowns; let laughter ring.
Revel in the joys of spring.
Fate's crueller blows may wound you so
It seems too much to bear,
But nought can slay the seeds of hope,
And if, like the seedlings, hope can grow,
Please God, - you'll cope.

While nature promises so much,
Enjoy it all the while we may.
Despite life's ups and downs and such,
Live for the essence of the day,
   --- And welcome spring.

IT'S BACK

Ah, - Summer. Season of wine and roses.
Sunshine and swimming.
All that slimming paying dividends around the pool.
Luscious cherries: succulent strawberries.
Tangy ice-cream, - oh, so cool.

Country lanes to stroll at leisure.
Sparkling streams and azure sky.
Summer, - time of joy and pleasure.
-- leave the chores till by-and-by.

In the coolness of the evening,
When the sun has gone to rest.
Jobs that perchance should not be leaving.
That' s the time to do them best.

Summertime, - so swiftly passing.
Let's enjoy each chance we find.
If, like me, you're well retired,
Business 'musts' are left behind.
Crowded trains and commerce queries
Done and dusted; sealed and signed.

So, gather ye rosebuds while ye may.
Enjoy the summer, every day,
-- And to yourself be kind.

MADE OF THIS

Seek not the past to light your days,
Tempting though that may be,
For naught can catch the golden haze
Of precious memory.

And to be sure none can erase,
Nor steal it from the heart.
'Tis the fabric of your life always,
Wove from the very start.

Yet as you travel on life's way
There are new chances every day
To do the things you long to do
And make your dearest dreams come true.

And in the process, to be sure,
Adding even more sweetness
To memory's store.

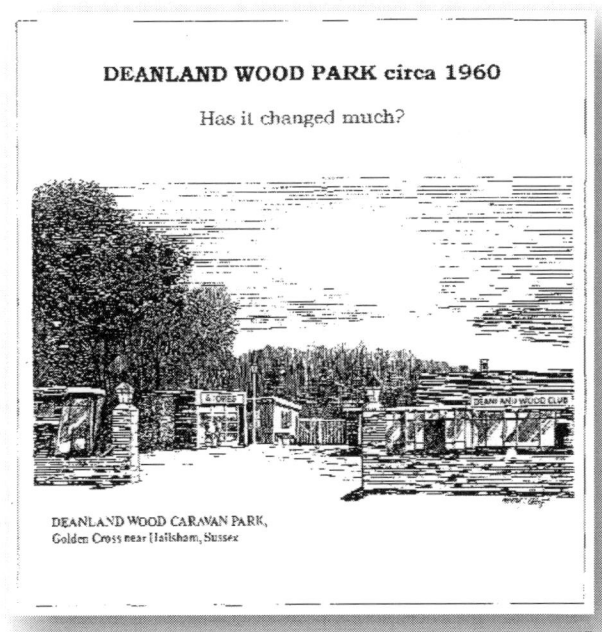

DEANLAND WOOD PARK circa 1960

Has it changed much?

DEANLAND WOOD CARAVAN PARK,
Golden Cross near Hailsham, Sussex

BUT NOT GOODBYE

Okay, Summer- if you have to go
Then go with our grateful praise
Go with our happy smiles for all the
Sunshine of your days

The blissful languor you bestowed
The flowers and the fetes
The cricket of the village green
The swimming with our mates

The glorious sunset, mellow moon
That made young blood run fast
The succulent fruits to please our tongue
Sea-shells and beaches for the young

Okay, summer- if your song is sung
Go, if you must, but take our trust
That you will surely reappear
To share your charms with us next year

THE SPIRIT OF CHRISTMAS

Greet it with a wondrous spirit,
0'er the hills and in the dells.
Greet it for the joy that's in it.
Greet the carols and the bells.

Greet it for its holy reason.
Greet its message of good cheer.
Greet this happy, happy season.
Send its tidings far and near.

Greet the family,
Friends and neighbours.
Everyone you chance to meet.
Let the joyousness of Christmas
Make yuletide happiness complete.

Spread the tidings here and yonder.
Foster well the warm goodwill.
Merry Christmastime is with us,
And its message lingers still.

CAROLS AROUND THE PARK
Tuesday 13th December 7.00pm

We will once again be going around the Park singing carols and raising money for the Macmillan Cancer Relief Fund.
We will be leaving the car park at 7.00pm, anyone welcome to come and sing. Your donation towards this very worthy cause will be much appreciated.

Barbara Roberts

DEANLAND SINGERS

Many thanks to all our friends and supporters who came to our Summer Show. The two performances raised an amount of £118.42. At present no decision has been made as to how this money will be allocated. As soon as a worthy cause has been decided upon, we will let you know.

Unfortunately due to unforeseen circumstances the Singers will not be presenting a Christmas Concert. Our next Concert will be on the 21st and 22nd January 2006, when we look forward to your continuing support.

Many thanks,
Joan Willis

ALZHEIMERS FUND RAISING
29.10.2005

Deanlanders you have done it again - £350.00 - raised on behalf of the above Society. I cannot thank you enough for your continuing generosity. I hope you all enjoyed our Musical Evening and I would once again express my sincere thanks to all my friends who did so much to ensure the evening was a success.

Eileen Ledger

2006 - 2010

I WONDER!

'Twas just gone midnight, New Year's Eve.
We were singing *'Auld Lang Syne'*.
I went outside to clear my head,
From drinking so much wine.

<u>Who</u> was that coming down the lane?
I closed my eyes, then looked again.
It wasn't anyone I <u>knew</u>.
I peered again, and wondered - who?

Who was that old man, tired and worn,
Walking with heavy tread?
With shoulders bent; a sorry sight
He seemed, on that moonlit winter night.

I called to him as he went by,
But he didn't stop, nor meet my eye.
I think be raised his arm a fraction,
But it was such a listless action.

I wondered whither he was bound,
And would he reach his goal.
He seemed exhausted, drained and spent.
I pitied the poor old soul.

But, at the corner of the lane,
A youth appeared. I looked again.
The essence, <u>he</u>, of vim and vigour.
Such contrast to the old man's figure.

I saw their meeting and their greeting.
The old man looked relieved.
Like a soldier with his duty done,
Or a prisoner reprieved.

I watched the young man help the old
Till they were out of sight.
But as I turned to go indoors and join my
Noisy friends.

The young man came in sight again,
Walking briskly along the lane.

--- And there my story ends. - <u>Except</u>,
I got to wondering, as one does at times
Like this. -- Was the tired old man 2005?
--- And the young, 2006?

I <u>know</u> I'd had a lot to drink, but - all the
same - it <u>makes</u> one think.

ALL IN THE AIR

Can't you hear it? - <u>Say</u> you hear it.
Don't let me be the only one.
I can't bear it lest you share it.
Don't say my time of reason's done.

Can't you feel it? - <u>Say</u> you feel it.
Like a frisson in the air.
Resting lightly; oh, so lightly,
All around and everywhere.

Can't you see it? - Say you see it.
Don't say this joy dwells just in me.
'Tis the time of life's renewing.
It's the glorious Spring, - you <u>see.</u>

SUCH A GARDEN

If our memories were planted,
What a garden they would make.
Brilliant blooms for our successes.
We could <u>rake</u> the odd mistake.

There'd be roses for remembrance,
Passion-flowers for romance.
All the happiness we've known
Would be there in the seeds we've sown,
And enchant our every glance.

There'd be an ornamental bridge
To span life's shifting stream,
And in the rippling waters
We could recollect each dream.

We'd revel in the heady scent
Of reminiscence, quite content.
The loves we've known would be full-grown
And like a sheltering tree.

Yes, - if memories were planted,
What a garden that would be.

DEANLAND SINGERS

To all our Deanland friends, we must once again express our sincere thanks for your continuing support.

We are combining the amounts raised by our Summer 2005 and January 2006 Concerts and will be donating the amount £300 between the two societies detailed below:

Sussex Air Ambulance   £200
Diabetic Society   £100

We think these are two very worthwhile charities and trust you will agree with our choice.

Our **Summer Concert** will be in August of this year and know that we can again rely on your support. Hope to see you all again then.

Joan Willis

ENJOY

There is no written guarantee.
One cannot stake a claim.
But you'll know when you have found it,
just the same.
It's there one minute, gone the next.
With you when you least expect.
Playing a funny, will-o'-the-wispy game.

You seek it here; you seek it there.
Just like that Pimpernel; everywhere.
Sometimes it seems just inches from
your grasp.
Then, suddenly, it's found you; in and out
and all around you.
And, when it's there, take handfuls in
your clasp.

Maybe a little demon's hovering,
It's called dissatisfaction.
Just spurn it with the scorn it so deserves.
Shrug it off and count your blessings.
There may be more than you have thought.
So many, there's a full team and reserves,

So, enjoy each magic moment.
Don't just take them all for granted,
For the more that you appreciate,
the deeper they'll be planted.
Well, that is that, then, more or less.
But you're ahead of me I guess.
I'm sure there's no need to remind you.
It's waiting there; just let it find you.
    -- HAPPINESS --

SPOILT FOR CHOICE

Life, it seems, is like the Seasons.
Sweet as <u>Spring</u> when you are young.
When everything is fresh and new,
And loving care embraces you.

<u>Summer</u> is a blaze of glory.
Epicentre of life's story.
Health and strength at peak and nothing
seems beyond your power.
All the world's your oyster and success
your favourite flower.

Then <u>Autumn</u>, - oh, kind Autumn.
Time to sit back and relax.
No more rushing to the office,
or the factory, or the Fax.
Time to travel; time to play;
time to savour every day.

And <u>Winter</u>, - gentle Winter.
Snowy ground and snowy hair.
Wondrous memories to dwell on from your
comfortable armchair.
But, life's story isn't over yet.
More pages there to turn, - you bet!

Yes, - life's phases, like the Seasons,
give us reasons to rejoice.
So, let us just enjoy them <u>all</u>.
That way we won't be spoilt for choice.

JUST THINKING

Think red, think white, think flowing beard.
Think merry twinkling eyes.
Think fun, think laughs, think happiness,
Then look up in the skies.

Think reindeer riding on the clouds
 with presents in their sled.
Then hang that stocking carefully,
 before you go to bed.

Think food, think drinks, think cards and gifts.
Think relatives and friends.
Think cosy rooms and fairy-lights,
 and joy that never ends.

Think of the blessings you have had,
 and, please God, those still in store.
Think mistletoe and 'Ho-Ho-Ho'.
The bells, the carols and the snow.

I'm <u>thinking</u>, <u>just</u> thinking; it <u>must</u> be --

> CHRISTMAS!!
> (Have a happy one!)

THE GATE OF THE YEAR   2007

They stood there, at the gate of the year.
Two stalwart, lifelong friends.
Bonded by shared experience
Of fortune's fickle trends.

One looked back to the road behind.
The other sighed, then said,
"There were traumatic times, it's true,
But we'd the strength to see it through.

And there was happiness as well.
Fate's soothing balm, I'd say.
One doesn't have to lose the past
To welcome the new day".

With arm half-raised against the light
One scanned the road ahead.
The other's smile was somewhat tight,
Though not a word was said.

Both shrugged. They knew the answer lay
In what transpired day by day.

They straightened up and, heads held high.
The New Year's gate flung wide,
Stepped boldly forward, side by side,
And <u>HOPE</u> walked with them; stride for stride.

(HAPPY NEW YEAR)

NONAGENARIAN NOTIONS

So, I am <u>90</u>. That means, if awake,
I could have seen the dawn breaking 32,872 times
(including Leap Years.) Now, that's a lot of
breaking, isn't it?

When I was young the mere thought of anyone
living to 90 made me and my pals roll about with
glee. And now that comical 90 thing is happening
to me.

And all <u>I've</u> done is just keep breathing in
and out, - or out and in as the case may be.
And though my outer face is running a losing race,
I still lay claim that I'm the same as I have <u>always</u> been,
beneath the wrinkled skin that now I'm in.

So, - here's to nonagenarians. May they
live to see the 'ton'. If the Queen Mother could
do it, why should the rest of us be outdone?

And just one more Nonagenarian notion, which
Is factual and true. The friendliness and happiness
I've found in Deanland has done much to see me through.

Thank you for everything.

CAROLS AROUND THE PARK
12 December 2006

I am extremely pleased to let you all know that we raised the magnificent sum of £463.11 for the Macmillan Cancer Trust. This is the best we have ever done, topping last years total by almost £50.00! My grateful thanks go to John and Ron for providing the music, the six stalwarts who knocked on doors and did their very best to sing along with the music, and last but by no means least to Dorothy & Tony Rumens and their friends who sent us on our way full of mulled wine, mince pies and sausage rolls. WELL DONE EVERYBODY!

Barbara Roberts

A note for your diary

The Deanland Entertainers will be putting on their annual show this year on Saturday, 21st April, and Sunday 22nd April. More details in next issue.

Annual General Meeting. The Annual General Meeting of the Deanland Wood Park Social Centre for members is to be held on Wednesday 24th October at 3pm in the Social Centre. Under the revised constitution the following positions will be filled at this meeting: Chairman, Vice-Chairman, Secretary, Treasurer and 4 members. The following members of the present committee will seek re-election – Geoff Stone, Charlie Measham, Jackie Carter, Kathie Page, Dorothy Rumens, Daisy Pragnell, Queenie Cornford & Sid Tomkins. If anyone wishes to be nominated to serve on the Social Committee, nomination forms are available from the Secretary Jackie Carter. Tel.   Completed nomination forms must be returned to the Secretary at 8, Fox Hollow by 10th October. Nominations will not be accepted after this date or at the meeting.

Any member wishing to raise a topic for discussion at the AGM MUST advise the Secretary (Jackie Carter, at the above address) in writing by 10th October at the latest.

Members only are entitled to vote at the AGM meeting so please bring your Membership Card with you so that membership can be checked at the door.

Your Membership can be renewed immediately after the conclusion of the meeting.

A LOVELY DAY

He said to her, "May I walk with you?"
She said, "I do not mind."
He said, "I love your eyes of' blue."
She said, "You're very kind."
He said to her, "May I know your name?"
She said, "It's Mary-Ann."
He said, "That's nice. I wonder, - would
  you let me hold your hand?"
She said, "You may, - on this lovely day.
On this <u>special</u> day you may."
He took her hand in his and they continued
  on their way.
He said to her, "On this lovely day; a
  <u>special</u> day, you mentioned. Do you think
  that at I might steal a kiss? Would you deem
  it well-intentioned?"
She looked at him a bit askance; yet there
  was laughter in her glance.
She murmured, "On a day like this - -", and,
  smiling, raised her lips to his.
And the sun shone down from an azure sky,
  and the world seemed hushed and still.
They were absorbed with one another,
  until a strong voice called out -- "<u>Mother</u>."
And there, beside the garden gate, the family
  was waiting ..
"Oh dear," she sighed, -- "<u>So many</u>!"
"Well," he said, -- "Three generations.
-- It <u>is</u> our Golden Wedding Day. Let's
  join the celebrations."

VERA

It's almost a year since Vera was here;
at home with her husband, Wal.
But every day, come what may,
Wal was there by her side.
Confirming the vow - in sickness & health.

A love that can't be denied.
Almost a year since Vera was here,
here with her Deanland friends.
But friendship is forever; that's
the beauty of its style.
It doesn't fade because you're
not together for a while.

And all of us who knew her
remembered Vera's smile.
Reminisce about her sparkling wit,
And think of all the laughter that
we shared when she was fit.
Her witty quips at Bingo, her
vitality at Darts.
It's very sure that Vera knew the
way to reach our hearts.

And, though it sadly grieves us, we
know she really had to leave us,
For her illness grew too much for
her to bear.
And I'm sure that you'll all join
with me in telling Wal and family
Simply just how very much we
care.
And how we hope our sympathy
will be as it is meant to be,
A little source of solace to Wal and
all the family.

MEMORIES 2008

Of all the joys this life can bring.
With all that we are blessed.
Surely the gift of memory
Holds sway there with the best.

Painting a fleeting picture
Of long-gone, well-loved things.
Bringing us, from out the blue,
Scenes from the life that once we knew.

Lifting our hearts if we're depressed
With thoughts of times that we loved best.
The little triumphs that we had; our most important days.
Those happy times are locked away in our memory-bank always.

And memories are always kind.
Block out all little 'blips', I find.
Only lifting the veil to show
The reminiscence we love so.

And the way we live our lives today
Will be tomorrow's memories.
Making the most of every minute
Will plant a happy memory in it.

So, take a trip down Memory Lane.
Relive those precious times again.
They're yours to hold and yours to treasure.
May your dearest memories live for ever.

YOU SEE?

The sun is warm upon my face.
The early-morning dew makes grass an
emerald shimmering lake
'Neath skies of sapphire blue.

My ears are filled with music
as the songbirds greet the day.
The blossoming trees scent the
gentle breeze.
And there, along the way, a rider trots
in splendid style,
And shares the radiance of the day with
a friendly nod and smile.

The rippling stream has a silvery gleam,
And from the hedgerows, fresh from sleep,
a myriad of tiny creatures peep.
And, like the cat that got the cream,
I revel in the joy of my surroundings
for a while.

My heart's as light as the day is bright.
Happiness fills me so.
There's no place I would rather be
Than where I am, because, you see,
It's Summertime, you know.

THE FLOWER OF FRIENDSHIP

So many lovely flowers grace a garden.
Imbuing joy and solace to the eye.
And how divinely the perfume, wafting
from a fragile bloom,
Bequeaths a new dimension to the azure
summer sky.

Yes, there are wondrous flowers in a garden.
Yet, even so, there's one that stands apart.
A precious bloom that always stays,
Through every season, all your days,
And dwells within the precincts of your heart.

No earthly storm or hurricane can bend it,
Life's slings and arrows firm its roots more true.
It is the transcendental Flower of Friendship.

May it flourish everlastingly for you.

More News

Congratulations to four of our ladies for receiving their badges in recognition of the sterling work they did in the **Women's Land Army and the Women's Timber Corps**, in those dark days of the 1940's

Jean Ball, Eileen Evans and Ellen Embery were all Land Army and Daisy Pragnell was a "Lumber Jill" in the Timber Corps.

There may well be others on the Park who have received badges for this work, congratulations to them as well; the ones named above are the ones we know about.

I thought the Charity Fete held on Primrose Acre on Saturday 19th July, was delightful. It was well organised by the Social Centre Committee with a different format based on several gazebos which made the stalls fairly weatherproof, should it start to rain, as it happened we had a fine day. Well done to all for raising such a good sum for charity.

DREAM-STREAM

By the sunlit, sparkling water, in the fullness of the day
Someone's son and someone's daughter,
idling the time away.
He so strong and lithe and handsome.
She so winsome and demure.
Blissful both in their surroundings.
Held in Nature's sweet allure.

There beside the whispering stream,
two young people rest and dream.
Where, oh where, do their minds wander,
as they lie there so serene?
Is he on a hero's journey; lance and armour at the Tourney?
She, in scented boudoir surely,
pondering the evening's jewellery?
Both fantasising on romance?
He to charm and she to dance?

Alas, no dreams can last forever. The young man stirs and
rubs his eyes; gives the girl a nudge, and sighs.
"Now, come on, Sis, an end to this.
The clock has beaten us, it seems.
There're cows to milk and fields to plough.
Let's get back to the here and now.
'Twill be <u>tomorrow</u>, it would seem, ere next we dream
beside the stream."

Happily they wend their way; serene in the life they know.
Yet, - is his head held that much higher? Hold her eyes a
deeper glow?
The sun shines down from a cloudless sky. The gurgling
stream flowing steadily by, sounds like somebody chuckling.
--- I wonder why!!

JOLLY HOLLY-DAYS

The other night I'm sure I heard, above the silver-frosted trees,
The sound of tinkling sleigh bells coming closer on the breeze.
And I was swept on memory's wings to days that used to be.
When I was young, and Dad and Mum and all the family
Were gathered there together, around the Christmas-tree.

Just for a moment I felt sad that such things were no more,
But a voice inside said, "Hey, - be glad, -- what are you grieving for?
Rejoice to have such memories. That love will never die."
I wiped away the tears and looked up at the starry sky.
I heard the tinkling bells again, and believe I saw the sleigh.
Such happiness is never lost. -- Hurrah! for Christmas Day.

Memories are life's store of joy that will forever stay.
May your Christmas be perfection, and all that you desire.
May the mistletoe do its special thing and laughter make the rafters ring.
May the crackers' jokes be great, and the wishbone find your plate.
And, if you do the Lottery, may your wins accumulate.
Oh, yes, -- and if you make the Jackpot; be that what fortune sends,
Tie a knot around your finger;. -- add me to your list of friends.
(Only joking! Half, anyway?)

MERRY CHRISTMAS!

MERRY MUSINGS   2009

Hope you had a happy Christmas. Doesn't it just fly past!
The bits of tree and tinsel clinging to the carpet are the things
that seem to last.
Did you party with relations? Did your heart-rate stand the test?
Sometimes emotions run amok when you don that
festive suit or frock, and tears can mingle with the smile if you've
not seen them for a while; - the ones you love the best.
The wonder of the Holy Birth; that is what gives the Yuletide
worth.
The Queen's speech and the groaning 'board.
The music and the chatter. The glowing children's faces. They're
the things that make it matter.

And now a fine New Year is here. New calendars;
new diaries; new resolutions.
New hope to find the right solutions in this
thrilling game of life we play, - each one of us
and every day.
And I know your wish will match with mine in
praying 2009 will bring us happiness to remember,
from January to December; and on through all the
years to come, - ad infinitum.

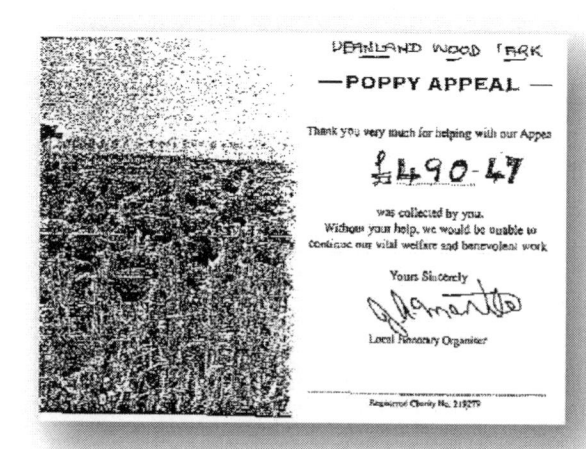

JUST THE THING

Like the inching upwards of a blind.
An urchin backing round a wall.
The fading sound of a seabird's call.
A taut spring starting· to unwind.
A good news easing of the mind.
Now is Winter left behind.

And in the earth and on the tree the
stirrings of new life you see.
The grass, so recent white with snow,
a brighter green than it's ever been.
And Nature's passing show begins to
gather and renew.

And all the dormant creature's too
are here again, and, there again,
The skies devise a deeper blue.
And there's a joy to everything.

------ SPRING!

THE DEANLAND ENTERTAINERS

A note for your diary!

The Deanland Entertainers will be **CONFUSED.DOT.COM** in the Social Centre on
Saturday 18th April at 2.30pm
Sunday 19th April at 7.00pm
Saturday 25th April at 7.00pm

Yes, three shows this time!

Entry programmes will be available from
Barbara at   Small Acre or Daisy at   Fox Hollow
Come along and join in the fun, music and laughter. Look forward to seeing you!!

Barbara Roberts

A MORNING STROLL

I met my friend, as had been planned,
an hour short of noon.
A morning stroll, you understand,
on a pleasant day in June.
Not a lot of conversation;
 just the odd word here and there.

For friendship such as ours well knew when silence
was the gold to share.
The sun upon our shoulders was soft as a caress.
And its rays danced lightly on the rippling brook.
The flowering hedgerows rustled as we were passing by, when
all the little creatures popped out to take
a look.

The blue sky filtered through the emerald canopy
of trees and brilliant butterflies danced everywhere.
My friend and I exchanged a smile and slowed our
progress for a while, to listen to the birdsong and
inhale the scented air.
And to watch a pony grazing in a field, quite unaware.
My friend exclaimed, with arms spread wide, "All this
beauty."
And I, ever down-to-earth, replied, "And it's free."
Then, as we turned our steps for home, refreshed quite
beyond measure,
We knew, however went the day; though it be toil or
leisure,
The memory of our morning stroll would be stored in
a box marked 'Treasure.'

A NICE DAY

The sun through the half-drawn drapes
was gentle on my face.
The birds' dawn chorus set me free from
Morpheus' embrace.
Isn't it lovely when summer is here.
Brighter days; lighter clothes; lighter chores.

Inviting outdoor things to do, when the
summertime temperature soars.
Go for a swim or lounge by the sea.
Walk in the country; scrumptious cream tea.
Relax in the garden amidst all the flowers
at the peak of their seasonal display.

Under a sheltering tree with a book.
Down by the river with sinker and hook.
Watching or playing your favourite sport;
bowls, tennis, cricket or such.
So much to do on a fine summer day the
choosing is almost too much.

Then the evening shadows fall and the sun
slowly sinks in the west.
The sky deepens to indigo and the birds
sleepily, cheepily fly to their nest.
The stars, like jewels on a velvet gown,
are winking, twinkling and bright.
And the amber moon hangs large and low,
seeming almost at shoulder height.

To All Residents

As many of you know I am your resident volunteer for East Sussex Hearing Resource Centre.

This is to let you all know that the Deaf Outreach Bus will be in our car park On 30th April. from 10.30am to 3.30pm.

On the Bus we offer advice on hearing problems and demonstrate equipment available to help the hard of hearing.
A hearing Screening test is available.

So if you or someone you know seems to be having difficulty hearing just come along for some free friendly advice.

It is planned to have a representative from Adult Social Services on board to offer help and advice to you regarding benefits and other help available to registered hard of hearing.

Hope to see you there as I will also be on the bus.

John Ward

For more information
Telephone 01323
E-mail:- mail@

Deaf Outreach Service

Deanland Wood Park
Golden Cross
Thursday 30th April 2009
10.30am—3.30pm

FREE advice and information on deafness

Provided by the East Sussex Hearing Resource Centre
in partnership with Adult Social Care

East Sussex Hearing Resource Centre
8 St. Leonard's Road, Eastbourne,
East Sussex, BN21 3UH
Tel. 01323 722505
E-mail: mail@eshrc.org.uk

For more information,
please visit:
www.eshrc.org.uk

Deanland Social Club presents...

OLDE TYME MUSIC HALL

Tuesday 29 September 2009 7.0pm

Your Invitation to Another Open Stage Night
of Acoustic Music at
"The Inn on the Park"
Deanland, Golden Cross.
Last Weds. Every Month at 8.30pm
All sorts of music: Folk, Country, Blues....
Singers & Musicians are welcome to sing and play.
Or just come and listen. Hope to see you there.
For anymore info call Jill on 01825

WORTH THE SEARCH

Has anyone seen my 'get-up-and-go'? I'm looking
for it far and wide. I know that I had it.
It was right here. That's something that can't be denied.

I'm missing it badly, but what can I do? It's hard
to remember when one's 92. But I'm going to persist
for it is sadly missed and I need it for seeing me through.

I'll go to bed early. Have regular meals. Find out
whether that does the trick. For all that I know
my 'get-up-and-go' is hiding; and that's a 'bit thick.'
I don't want to lose it. I still need to use it.
It's awfully important to me. Of course it is not so
strong as it was. One couldn't expect it to be.
But, nevertheless, I miss it because without it
life's boring, you see.

But, wait just a mo', I'm feeling a glow. Can it
be that I'm on the right track? Don't look any more,
it's just come in the door.
Yes, - my 'get-up-and-go' has come back!

Birds are singing. Sun is shining. No more grumbling;
no more whining. I'll leave those foolish things out
in the cold. My taste buds are peaking. It's the
'good life' I'm seeking. After all, 92 isn't really
<u>that</u> old!

Oh! My 'get-up-and-go' has had something to say.
It whispered these words in my ear. It said, "If you
use me there's no fear you'll lose me. Employ me
each day and I'll stay."
     ---Hooray!!

THAT TIME AGAIN

Parties and pantomimes. Gifts around the tree.
Lights and decorations. Fun and fantasy.
Something streaked across the sky.
Could it be a sleigh?
And isn't that a 'Ho-ho-ho' echoing across the snow?
Who's to venture yea or nay this close to Christmas Day?
Mum's making a trifle and Dad's trimming the tree.
Auntie's sitting, smiling, with the baby on her knee.
Uncle's reading all the cards and fondly reminiscing.
Ross and Jen are in the hall, where the mistletoe is
hung. (What it is to be in love and young!)

The children are revising their lists to Santa Claus,
and the cat behind the sofa is keeping a hypnotic eye
on an unguarded mince-pie.
Mum's smiling eyes are shining, 'though she's only
had one sherry (supposedly!) Hope the trifle's not
gone short. (Perish the thought!) Dad's fighting a
fairy-light. Was that a little swear? Mum wouldn't
care for that, especially with the children there,
but smilingly says not a word, just as if she hasn't
heard. (It's really difficult to stifle qualms re.
sherry reaching trifle!)

Carollers are at the door, singing loud and clear.
Everybody goes outside to proffer festive cheer.
Mother's face is all aglow. Dad leads her to the
mistletoe!
The moon shines palely on the snow. Can't you hear
that 'Ho-ho-ho'?

May the happiness of Christmas in every home abide.
And be a close companion long after Yuletide.

SOUNDS GOOD TO ME   2010

Hope the festive season was O.K. and up to
expectations.
Plenty of happy moments with dear friends
and relations.
Now 2009 has had its day; I know just how
that feels.
But, Hey! 2010 is here, - snapping at its
heels.
A new year, full of promise. Does it fill
your heart with vigour?
Depending on one's age it's maybe 'some and
some', I figure.

Each year is like a journey; let's say – on a train.
May your hand-luggage consist of hope and
health and happiness, and any sad things
that persist be bundled in the guard's van
and then in 'Lost Luggage' remain.

2010 has a special ring. I hope that you agree.
10th year of the millennium, and may it prove
to be a year that we'll remember with heartfelt
joy and pride.
That is my New Year wish for you, and everyone
beside.

2010 sounds good to me. Let it be!

IT'S SPRING, YOU SEE

We were standing in the garden, beneath a
blossoming tree, 'midst crocuses and daffodils;
Spring's glorious legacy. -- My friend Mary and me,
And the shimmering dazzle of the sun from the
bluest of blue skies could not outshine the sparkle
in my friend Mary's eyes. She was in love!

Mary isn't a young woman; rather more than mature;
but young-at-heart and well-esteemed by everyone who
knew her·.
Her husband died a while ago. Their love had been
sublime,
Is this, I wondered pensively, - can this be the
time she's found another soulmate; someone to care
and share?
After we'd chatted for a while she said that she must
Leave. And, oh, the radiance of her smile, - who
could believe!
I watched her walking down the lane, turned away, -
then looked again,
Where there was one; now there were two; hand-in hand,
moving out of view.
It's Spring, you see!
The season when sweet romance takes a hold.
It matters not to Cupid whether one is young or old,
And love is not the only thing that's nurtured by the
season. For Nature seems to sound a waking call.
And from her bounteous larder the good things she
bestows are indeed a boon and blessing to us all, -
because, - It's Spring, you see.

POPPY APPEAL

Thank you very much for helping with our Appeal.

£464-70p

was collected by you.
Without your help, we would be unable to
continue our vital welfare and benevolent work.

Yours Sincerely

Local Honorary Organiser

Registered Charity No. 219279

Deanland's Got Talent

Performing on the TV show Britain's Got Talent, Jean & Terry McEwan (with a combined age exceeding 160) received a standing ovation from the 3 judges for their rendering of *Let It Be Me* at the Hammersmith Apollo in London and went through to the second round of the competition. As Terry said, "We were staggered when everyone in the entire theatre stood up and clapped for us. It was a memorable experience." And Jean added, "I think we're good enough at singing – maybe we let ourselves down during the interviews'." From the thousands of hopefuls that performed, some 400 were put through to the second round but, unfortunately, only a select few made it to the live TV finals. And Jean and Terry did not make it.

Well done to you both, Deanland is proud of you.

Just to dispel any rumours that may be going around the Park following Dad's death: **The family is not selling The Park; nothing is changing for the present.** Our Mother, who is 90 this year, is still alive, albeit in a nursing home, so we need to consider her and she could live to be a hundred!

Keith Whitehead

SCIENTIFICALLY PROVEN

It was in the Science-Lab. that he and she first
met. Both of them were just 16. They shared a
Bunsen-burner, and he passed her a pipette.
And, when they used the microscope, heads close
above the lens, his youthful heart was in a whirl,
and it was very clear the <u>girl</u> was in no way aloof;
that is, of course, if blushing cheeks can be
acclaimed as proof. And that ever-watchful Cupid;
- the science of love his art, had found a perfect
target for his ever-ready dart.

And, oh, the world was bright for them, and everything
seemed just right for them. Two young people,
just by chance, in the enchantment of romance.
Until there dawned that dreadful day; the day when
they first heard her family must move away. Her
father's job had been transferred!

When the time came they were bereft, and vowed they'd
ne'er forget; from dawn until the sun was set, from
January to December; and he drew from his pocket a
charming little silver locket, which he gave her, -
to remember!

Time passed, and it was 20 years before they met again.
<u>She</u> was meeting a friend at the station, when <u>he</u>
stepped off the train.
They knew each other instantly, despite the passing
years. Both happily wed, with families. Still, it
was a poignant scene; mixture of laughs and tears.

They reminisced on times gone by, and he said, with a
little sigh, - "I don't suppose, -- I mean --?"
She smiled, and from about her throat drew forth the
locket, which she'd cherished all the years between.
There was no duty to explain. No apologies to make.
They knew that both had kept their troth, 'though
life itself had channelled both in a different direction.
Now they could go <u>on</u> again; happy in the memory of
that sweet teenage affection.

SO NICE

On a seat beside the sea, beneath a sun-drenched sky.
Two ladies getting on in years watching the world go by.
Comfortable together; friends from childhood days.
Old friends like old wine are the best, or so
the adage says. Cloudless sky and sparkling sea.
For sure, a pleasing place to be. Resting a while
after their stroll their contentment complete, on that
oh so welcome, strategically sited splendid seaside seat.
They smiled to see the children playing on the beach.
The parents watching them with loving care. The
paddlers and the swimmers.
The laughter, shrieks and yells. The canoodling young
sweethearts and the lovely bathing-belles. The beaming
satisfaction when a child found special shells.

Cont...

The gatherings round the ice-cream seller.
Now <u>there's</u> a mighty popular fella!
The strains of well-loved music from the bandstand
further on. The wheeling gulls competing with their cry.
Is it feelings of nostalgia that makes our ladies sigh
and wipe a little moisture from the eye?

Do they dwell for just a moment on the years that have gone, when their families were young and they themselves would be the centre of the laughter and the fun? But look, their smiles are bright again and of course it is a friend's domain to share the pleasure and the pain. And it's nice to take things easier than they did when they were young and when it was <u>their</u> spring song that was sung. The ladies exchanged a glance; a little raising of the brow. Expressions seeming to convey, - well, that was <u>then</u>, and this is <u>now</u>.

One says, - "It's been a lovely day." The other, - "I agree. I really have enjoyed it. It's <u>so nice</u> by the sea." They rise as one with the setting sun and continue on their way. Next stop, - a cup of tea? Now, you might well be wondering, - or not, as the case may be, - how I know so much about them. Well, you see; One of them is my friend Vi, - and the <u>other</u> one is <u>me</u>.

SLIPPERY SAM

Slippery Sam was in a jam. He really was quite sweet.
But, try as he may, in every way, all through the night and
through the day, he couldn't control his feet.
He tried so hard to make them go in his desired direction.
But, though he tried to be discreet, the moment he rose to his
feet, he'd slip and slide from side to side in uttermost dejection.

He slithered to the north or south when he wanted east
or west. His foot was really in his mouth. He couldn't
come to rest; and thought and pondered as he wandered, -
what to do for the best?

People claimed he'd had too much to drink, as he went
sliding by. Oh, what a foolish man, they'd think;
raising their eyes towards the sky. They didn't see
Sam's silent plea; the anguish on his face.
They stepped aside in their alarm, whereas a kind, restraining
arm would have stopped Sam's headlong pace.
Sam soled his shoes with sandpaper, and anything that
gripped. But nothing seemed to stop the slide; nothing
he did controlled the skid, so Sam, poor Sam, - still slipped.

Now, - you will realise, of course, Sam isn't really real.
In these enlightened days some genius would, as well he
should, bring Slippery Sam to heel.
But, ere I put poor Sam away, in my itsy-bitsy box, I will
just tell you of the day a pretty maiden came his way,
with glorious golden locks.

Sam, from the corner of his eye, saw her as he went sliding
by, and stopped as though someone had slammed a brake.
He gazed at her, - and she at he. Oh, it was really
meant to be. Sam pinched himself to see he was awake.
She took Sam's arm with gentle charm. Sam's slithering
days were over. Now she and he live happily, in wedded
bliss, - in clover.   (In my little box!)

THE HAMPER   *(From a young man to his family at Christmas)*

Dear Mum and Dad,
I won't be home for Christmas due to orders from above.
The head of my Department to be plain. For my name
was on the roster and as I saw it coming up my hopes of
being with you all went sliding down the drain.
But I had a good idea, and this <u>hamper</u> is the theme,
as each item it contains brings thoughts of you.
So I <u>will</u> be there at Christmas even though just in my
mind and I know that you'll be thinking of me too.

In my hamper there's a turkey, which I hope you will
enjoy, and that engenders memories of when I was a boy.
For Dad '<u>talked turkey</u>' to me when I didn't 'toe-the-line'.
And put me on the 'straight and narrow'. - I was about 9.
Then, of course, there are the cheeses. I hope that my
selection pleases. Strong Cheddar and soft Brie. Just
the way you were with me, and, of course, with all the
others in the family. Strong when it was needed, but
soft and loving too. How apt it is the foods of life
should bring me close to you. Even with the chocolates;
some are soft and some are hard. But always <u>sweet</u>, like <u>you</u>.

That's why you're held in such regard. The ham and tongue;
well, when I was young I 'hammed it up' a bit. And the
'tongue' was when you put me back in the right way of it.
And the jam and jellies, fruit and cream were like our
happiness. And the pickles were our little setbacks here
and there, I guess! And the 'crackers', well, they signify
our joyful merriment. So the contents of this hamper leave
me feeling quite content. Though I'm mixed-up, like the
pudding, it's been money quite well-spent. Oh, I nearly
forgot the vintage wine, and that will never do. For I
know you'll drink a toast to me, as I'll surely do to you.
Love, Tim,

> P.S. Oh, by the way, I've heard today that I <u>won't</u> be 'on call'.
> So your loving son will share the hamper with you after all.

Just a reminder
Of summer

The Inn On The Park
Deanland Wood park
Golden Cross
Hailsham
East Sussex
BN27 3RR

SUMMER BBQ SWIM

Raising money for St Wilfred's Hospice

Join us for a fundraising event on **Saturday 15TH August 2009** at The Inn on the park.

Tickets are priced at £5 per person.
This ticket price includes a donation of **£3.50 to St Wilfred's Hospice** and £1.50 to the Inn on the park to cover the cost of food.

Tickets entitles the customer to One item from the BBQ,
Which will be a choice of Beef Burger, Hotdog or Chicken
Plus Pasta salad.

Event starts from 5pm till late, with Fun Bingo, Raffles, Games and More.... And if it's a beautiful evening don't forget to bring your swimwear.

Come Rain or shine this event will not be interrupted.

Plus music
From
Johnny Wakelyn

Tickets are available from the bar
Thank you

01825 872406

2011 - 2017

SPOTLIGHT ON – Deanland Men's Chorus

The Men's Chorus was formed by Geoff Stone just over 2 years ago. They meet once a fortnight for rehearsal and, in that time, have put together a wide repertoire of songs. Occasionally they put on an audience-riveting (not my words), foot-stomping show. They have performed as far away as Hailsham !! Their next performance is Sunday 13 February in the Social Centre, start 3.0 pm. So come along and listen and give them some support. (PS. New chorus members are always welcome - just an ability to sing a few notes and enjoy good company are the only requirements. Have a word with Geoff.)

DEANLAND ENTERTAINERS SHOW 2011

Once again the time has come round to announce our forthcoming show!

This year we will be performing on -
Friday 8th April at 7.00pm
Saturday 9th April at 2.30pm
Sunday 10th April at 7.00pm

We are keeping the title of the Show 'under wraps' at the moment but we hope you will be pleasantly surprised!
Many thanks for your support in the past and we look forward to seeing you all in April.
More information concerning tickets, etc. at a later date.
Many thanks
Barbara Roberts

Deanland Volunteer Car Service
Lifts to –

*Doctors Surgery   * Hospital   *Chiropodist
*Ports   *Opticians   *Dentist
*Airports   *Bus & Railway Stations

Please give as much notice as possible
Telephone

MEG'S CHOICE

Some time ago, when she was young; and comely too,
'twas told, Meg had three loves; all, I assure, cast
in a goodly mould. And all three loved her fervently,
and yearned to share her life. And each extolled
most urgently Meg's future as his wife.

The first was Raymond, - only son. So suave and
debonair. His father owned a factory. And houses -
everywhere. Fair turned Meg's head with all his talk
of holidays and jewels. Of nannies, maids and
governesses, and swanky private schools. Meg almost
answered 'Yes' right there. It seemed <u>the</u> thing to do.
But then, like something from the air, -remembered <u>No,2</u>.

Garth, he was called. A fitness freak. <u>Tarzan</u> had
nothing in it. Each time Meg glanced at his physique
she had to rest a minute. With her beside him as his
bride their life would be worth seeing. They'd
mountain-climb, Garth said, and ride. Go swimming,
skating, ski-ing. It was a dazzling prospect. All that
<u>muscle</u>, you'll agree. Meg nearly pledged her troth right
then. But -- <u>What of No.3</u>?

Edwin. - the perfect gentleman. A scholar, - so well-read.
Meg never ceased to marvel at the clever things he said.
They'd sit beneath the trees, Ed promised, and soliloquise.
And Chaucer, Keats and Shakespeare would evolve before
their eyes.
Wealth; health, and education. Gain <u>one</u> - and two to <u>lose</u>.
In such a situation, how <u>was</u> a girl to choose?

Then suddenly, as ne'er before, Meg's heart controlled her
head. She knew that <u>Bill</u> - <u>the boy next door</u> - was whom
she longed to wed. Her heart chose well; Bill loved her
true. They <u>wed</u>; thus ends this tale. A postman. Knew his
<u>letters</u>, too! Meg's <u>very</u> own <u>mail</u> male!

LOVE WAS THERE

Almost ere one is aware, it's there! All around
the spring is springing. Season of a new beginning.
Daffodils and blossoming trees enchanting every glance.

Brighter skies and lighter hearts and, maybe, perchance
- romance? For there's really nothing like the spring
to set that Cupid on the wing. And whether one be
young or old love's own sweet story can be told.

And love was there on that village green on that glorious
day in spring. Beneath the tree where they'd first met.
Their anniversary tree, you see. Under the boughs
where they'd made their vows and on her finger he had
set a beautiful diamond ring.

Love was there in their smiling eyes and hands so
fondly clasped. Were they drifting back in memory to
shared joys of the past? The happiness of times gone by? Maybe
even to the day their first-born bairn proffered his new-born cry?

Love was there as they turned toward their cottage down
the lane. Next year, I trow, if fate allow, they'll stand beneath
their tree again.
And, as the strengthening April sun glints the silver
In their hair, 'twould not be easy to deny, - even should
one elect to try, - that love was there.

--- Isn't it everywhere?

NICE 'N EASY

The necessary chores done, some hours of leisure
beckoned. Out in the garden in the sun would suit
me well, I reckoned.
So in a comfy lounger 'neath a blue and cloudless sky,
that is where I settled and let time go drifting by.
Now it isn't hard to please me but to take things
nice and easy I s'pose comes rather high upon my list;
and to sit there at my ease with a novel on my knees
came very close to almost perfect bliss.

I rested there content in the soft warmth of the sun,
with nature's burgeoning beauty all around. The
blossom-scented air was sweet beyond compare, and the
singing of the birds was like a joyous backing-sound.
And in that peaceful garden on that glorious summer's
day it seemed a touch of heaven had just chanced along
my way.

In fact, were I extremely rich and in a mansion dwelt,
there couldn't be more happiness than was right there,
I felt.

That was <u>nice,</u> - and I was <u>easy</u> with it. - - z z z z z z.

EVENTIDE

As the sun sinks low into the west; its daytime
duty through.
And the sky becomes a masterpiece of crimson,
gold and blue.
When the songbird's repertoire is stilled,
as he seeks his cosy nest.
And the squirrels cease their scampering,
whilst settling down to rest.
As the cattle in the meadow succumb to their
couch of green.
And an amber crescent moon above the soaring trees
is seen.
When the brilliance of the blossoms that, by day,
delight our sight.
As dusk descends weave gradually with the shadows
of the night.
When, along with the setting of the sun, the daytime
jobs have all been done.
And you step outside to be part of it.
The fragrant, beauteous heart of it.
The stillness wraps around, soft as a shawl.
As nature, even slumbering, adds enchantment to it all.
More wondrous, e'en, than words can say. --
A garden, -- at the close of day.

A WHISPER OF WHIMSEY

I said to my friend Mavis, "Do you feel a
certain chill rise from the lawn at early morn
'though summer has not long been gone?"
She said, "Yes, - I know just what you mean,
and, have <u>you</u> noticed, too, that although the
leaves are still quite green there is a sense
of faltering. <u>They</u> know the season's altering.
And they're aware, as <u>we</u> are, that everything
must change. They have their fond farewells
to make. Their <u>wardrobes</u> to arrange."
I felt a bit hysterical; should have <u>known</u>
that she'd wax lyrical.

She said, "If <u>you</u> were a leaf, drifting from a
tree, which colour do you think <u>you'd</u> like to be?"
I said, "Oh dear, what a question. I'd be in a
quandary. There's russet, yellow, gold and red,
to mention but a few. Be best if I could stay
there on the tree, I think, - don't <u>you</u>?"
She lost her other-worldliness like the dropping
of a hat, then laughed at me and said, "Fat
chance of that."
I said, "Mother Nature's wonderful. That
no-one can deny, and she's sent <u>me</u> a message
<u>too</u>, so what I plan to do is go and find myself
a cosy cardi. See you later, Mave, - Goodbye!"

ALWAYS

Nell and Tom were reminiscing on one snowy
Christmas-Eve. Drowsily, before the fire.
Nell gently touched Tom's sleeve.
"Do you <u>remember,</u> Tom," she said, "the day when
we first met?"
Tom peered at her across the hearth. "<u>Girl</u>, -
<u>how</u> could I forget?"
Neither said another word but smiles transformed
their faces as memory took them through the years
to other times and places.
The power of memory, you see, gave back to them
what used to be. No longer were they as today,
and very old, and frail, and grey.
<u>He</u> saw his Nell, a <u>lovely</u> lass, with hair like
shimmering gold. <u>She</u> saw her Tom, a handsome lad;
straight-limbed and proud and bold.
And then Nell touched Tom's arm again, and leant a
little nearer. Tom slowly wiped his spectacles, so
he could see her clearer.
Nell said, "It's nice to reminisce." Tom said, "Yes, I agree.
Come on, old girl, give us a kiss and cuddle up to me."
And through the sparkling windows the moon glistening
on the snow, and the evening-star shining from afar
filled the room with a cosy glow.

Cont........

And Nell and Tom, who, as I've said, were really <u>very old</u>,
sat there in perfect harmony. Happy as they could ever be.
Wrapped in the warmth of memory.
That wondrous cloak of gold.
And the tests and trials they'd had to weather, in all
the years they'd been together, were gone as though
they'd never been, for love is supreme on memory's screen.
So, at this festive season may the joys come thick and
fast, and in their wake, leave memories that will last
and last and last.

DEANLAND

December 2011

Welcome to the Christmas edition of the Deanland News. Last time round it was with great pleasure that I was able to announce that we'd won Park of the Year 2011, by now I'm sure most of us have seen the write up in the Park Home Magazine. Whilst not factually correct with all of their text, I think the photos of the Park and the sentiment behind it did us all justice. Thank you for all the suggestions of how best to spend the prize money. Some were very personal, some would cost £1000s, but many wanted us to find a way of marking the heritage of the park. With that in mind we are going to investigate the cost of a quality Spitfire weather vane to be placed at the entrance, possibly on the roof of the Inn. Hopefully they'll be enough leftover to buy at least one more memorial bench to go alongside the refurbished boules court and some new bird/bat boxes for the woodland walk; two more worthy suggestions given to us by other residents.

More good news, it has been officially announced that landraise is no longer to be considered as a waste option for the low weald by East Sussex County Council. This means that the land behind our field opposite the entrance to the park is no longer at risk to a landraise development. For peace of mind we have retained the legal team that keep an eye on these matters for us, in the short term at least!

THIS AND THAT   2012

It seems quiet after the Christmas rush and
all the hullabaloo.
The carols and the parties and the myriad things to do.
The meetings and the greetings and the festive
bonhomie.
At least, - it does to me.

I was asking my friend Mavis whether she felt
the same. She said she did, and reckons these
dark evenings are to blame. ·
We both agreed though that we thought they had a
certain charm; especially if one's indoors in the
warm. With a good book or the telly and the
household chores all done. Not much need, we
thought, to grieve the early setting sun.
Mave's a bit poetic, so she went on to say,
"Swift as the shadows fall comes a stillness over
all. And as the darkness heads our way a
deepening hush cossets the closing day."
We sat quietly for a minute, her and me, just
drinking our tea.

But, hey! How about this grand New Year we're
venturing along! Wherein our faith and hope and
trust presides. It's bound to have its ups and
downs as destiny decides. Laughs and tears as
in all years; but may fate so set the seals
that peace and health and happiness over all
prevails.

WHY JUST DREAM?

My friend Alice said to me, "I like the spring, don't you?"
I looked at her. "You know, " she said, "In spring
the whole world's <u>new</u>."
I thought, 'Oh dear' - it must be love, - she's not
usually poetic, - but Alice just gave me a shove
and said, - "Oh, you're pathetic. Don't you admire
the daffodils? The new lambs all a-leaping?"
I said, "Alice, - do you feel all right? You getting
enough sleep in?"
She said, "D' you mean to say the scent of hay leaves
you devoid of feeling?"
I said, "Oh, dear, - it's bad I fear." But she
looked so appealing. I said, "There's you and me stood
here in the middle of the city. No fields, no streams,
- it's only dreams, and that's the nitty-gritty.
No flaming daffodils around; no hay to stir the senses.
No leaping lambs or anything. Just factory walls, -
<u>not</u> fences."

She said, "I know all that, of course, but you see, on
the 'telly' there was this farmer and his horse, and
it really got to me; the trees and fields and
everything. It all looked so serene. It made me
wish that I was there, if you know what I mean."

Cont.

And as I looked at my friend's face, and saw her eyes
a-glowing; like her, I saw another place. "Alice,"
I said, - "We're <u>going</u>. We'll have to wait a little
while, till our holiday is due, but we'll go into the
country for a fortnight, me and you. We'll leave
behind the traffic noise and all the factories, and
savour all the country joys; the meadows and the trees.
It won't be spring, but summer too has its full share
of charms; with emerald fields and skies of blue, and
cottages and farms. And, so our dreams won't go away,
let's book our holiday today."

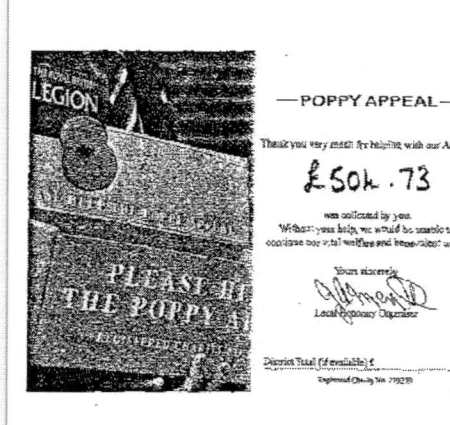

                     -- And we <u>did</u>.

POPPY APPEAL

Thank you very much for helping with our Appeal.

£504.73

was collected by you.
Without your help, we would be unable to
continue our vital welfare and benevolent work.

Yours sincerely,

Local Poppy Organiser

District Total (if available): £

Registered Charity No. 219279

15th February at 1.30pm

Please come to a presentation
of slides and a talk given by the
Revs. Jim and Mary Smith of
'The Serving Africa Mission'.
This is to alert us to the need of a
school for poor children in Accra,
Ghana.
There will be refreshments and an
opportunity for question at
approx. 3pm.

Lilian Ashby
Fellowship Group

The 2012 Entertainers show "A NIGHT ON THE TOWN" was performed to full houses at each show and great feedback has been received! We are so pleased everyone enjoyed it. We understand there were some sound issues, especially on our first night, and so this year we will be investing in some new microphones as we want to make sure the audiences for our next production can hear every word! We will also be sending a donation to two charities in the near future - details of which will be in the next Deanland News. Thank you <u>all</u> for your continued support. And talking of support, we are always looking for new people to join the Entertainers so if any of you out there would like to join us we would be very happy to see you. Our next get together will be at 2pm on Wednesday 25 July in the Social Centre - do please come along! Thank you to all once again!

Pat Richings

A JOLLY FINE SHOW

For two or three hours of sheer enjoyment one
would have been hard-pressed to find anything
better than the Deanland Entertainers' show,
'A Night on the Town.'

From start to finish it was undiluted pleasure,
as I' m sure all who saw it will whole-heartedly
agree.
The Entertainers merit the highest praise for their
selflessness in the amount of time and effort put in
to make the show such a success.
The stage-setting was sophisticated; the sketches
a 'hoot', and the music and songs appealing.

Not least of the enjoyment is the pride and pleasure
one feels in seeing friends and neighbours acting
with such skill, talent and aplomb. Speaking
personally, it made me feel quite 'puffed-up' to be
part of such a community.

It's said that laughter is a tonic and music a balm.
Certainly was the case for me.
Thank you, 'Deanland Entertainers,' so very much.

A LAKESIDE LYRIC

It had been a glorious day; late summer, don't you see.
And everywhere as warm and bright as it could ever be.
They'd strolled right round the sparkling lake,
- and that was quite a walk.
Admired the swans' majestic glide; enjoyed a quiet talk.
Now they were on a lakeside seat.
Thankful to rest their hard-pressed feet.
They didn't meet so often now, - and here's the reason why.
The distance between their homes seemed longer as the years rolled by.
But time and distance couldn't break the bond between these two,
With the lifetime's shared joys and sorrows they had both been through.
One closed her eyes and in a while her friend saw with a smile that Morpheus held her in her gentle arms.
Whilst she herself sat, quite content, - beside the lake, beneath the trees, enjoying nature's charms.
Too soon, though, it was time to go.
And, as they reached the spot which marked the parting of their ways,
One said, "I felt a breath of <u>heaven</u> there."
Said the other, "<u>So</u> did I."
And the sun burst forth in a golden blaze
as it sank in the western sky.

A BIT BATTY

In this year 2012 I've found a tendency to delve
into the realms of memory, and idly meandering
through drew this from 1932.

Captain of Ladies' Cricket, me, in the school where
I was at.
Mind, the pitch was hard, - a concrete yard, - but
we soon got used to that!
No club-house, but the bike-shed served as our
headquarters. We took such setbacks in our stride, -
us doughty cricketing daughters.

No namby-pamby underarm in the matches that we played.
Over-arm and hard and fast. We ladies weren't afraid.
We didn't score a lot of runs. Centuries a wishful dream.
But in our school our cricketing prowess
christened us 'the cream.'
And we were young and in our prime. The joys of
spring and everything.

That, though, was 80 years ago. Switch to today,
you'd see ----- Old woman in an armchair, cradling a
cup of tea!

Deanland Stores & Golden Cross Post Office

A Time for Change

With effect from Monday 1 October we will be handing over to the new owners, Martin, Sue and Michael Long. This is proving to be difficult to write, but we do so with happy and sad feelings, so let's get the sad ones out of the way first.

We are getting older and are feeling extremely weary, having worked 60 – 70 hours a week for the past 5 years. There have been times of sadness at the passing of some true characters who we had grown fond of. We have shared troubles and woes with many. We will miss so many of you who come in every day and give us a bit of cheek – you are our extended family.

Of course as in any place and time there will be instances that make you chuckle, and we have had many. We often grab a pen and write down some things (there may be a book one day). Here are a few examples of how our days have gone.

"Has my Betterware come in yet?"
"What did you order?"
"One of them scrubbers for the shower and one of them covers for your dubries"
"Sorry, they're not in yet, it'll be next Wednesday."

Another day, another customer:
"The Gardener's coming to cut the grass. I've got some ginger nuts but he also likes those cakes – the German ones beginning with K. Oh here they are – Tirimasou."

At the Post Office a customer asked if Pete would mind signing a form for him.
"No problem" he replied.
"Thanks, it will save me going and knocking a neighbour up."

One lady brought her newspaper up to the counter, offered payment and pointed to the headline, "Every day there's something different isn't there."

Needless to say we have have loads of laughs as well as befriending many people at Deanland and from the surrounding area.

On a happy note we are looking forward to a few weeks away – Dorset and Devon are beckoning, as are the fishing rod and the sewing box. We hope to return refreshed and raring to go -- to see what the next chapter in life will bring us.

We thank all our customers for making the last 5 years a time we will look back on with happy memories and trust you will welcome Martin, Sue and Michael and that they will serve you well.

Just to confirm to you all, the shop will be open from 8.30 – 12 noon on Monday 1 October, then closed for the afternoon to allow for the stocktake. Peter will hand over the Post Office on Tuesday 2 October when the new owners will welcome you.

You truly are a special group of people and it's been a pleasure doing business with you.

Gill.   *Pete.*
(I cried writing this)   (You daft softie)

THE CLOAK

May the spirit of Christmas enwrap you like a cloak.
A garment woven on the loom of love.
With the silken threads of friendship and the
cotton of compassion.
And a quilted lining filled with laughter.
Soft as a turtle-dove.

May every shining button reflect your dearest dreams.
And may the really <u>special</u> ones come true.
And may the roomy pockets be bursting at the seams.
So full are they with happiness for you.

May it rest upon your shoulders as light as thistledown.
Yet have the power to warm you through and through.
And may the joys of Christmas be with you every day.
With this special cloak the angels made for you.

<u>Happy Christmas</u>

OH, BLOW!   2013

Oh, there goes the doorbell. Wonder who it
  can be. I'll go and find out in a mo, - when I've
  drunk this cup of tea.

If this armchair weren't so cosy I'd go now, just
  to be nosey. But it is, so I won't. World won't
  end if I don't.
Could be nice to have a chat 'bout one thing or
  another. But curiosity killed the cat, so p'raps
  I just won't bother.

Oh, there goes the bell again. Talk about
  obstinate. Now he's calling through the letterbox.
Well, that's rude, - so he can wait. ·
He said, "Seems I've the wrong address, so I'll be
  on my way. My name is OPPORTUNITY."
"Oh,- no," I cried. "Please stay."

I rushed pellmell across the room and flung the
  door wide. Too late! Too late! No-one was there.
Nobody was outside.
Searched far and wide and high and low.
--- Oh, Blow!

Dear All,

Many, many thanks for your wonderful support at our Christmas Carol Concert which took place at the Inn on 4 December. As you may know all proceeds from the concert were given to St Wilfrid's Hospice in Eastbourne, where I regularly volunteer. I was absolutely delighted to hand over the following: £102.70 collected for teas, coffees and mince pies - and thank you very much Karl and the team for supplying these items free of charge, very much appreciated by one and all. £265 from the raffle - and again your generosity knows no bounds for all the fantastic prizes that were donated. Finally £87 was collected for the "memory stars" that were hung on the Christmas tree. So all in all we collected £454.70 and well done and thank you sooooooooo much, St Wilfrid's were delighted to receive this amount.

Everyone who came along to the concert thoroughly enjoyed it and the atmosphere was lovely. Well done too to all those who participated in the three choirs, it was an absolute pleasure to be part of such an enjoyable event.

Love and thanks again
Pat Richings

SEASONAL SOLILOQUY

I love the sharp and tingly air that Winter brings.
Snuggling in an armchair with woolly socks and things.
I love Summer's warm embracement and outdoor fun.
The softly blossom-scented evenings when the day is done.
I love the Autumn, even with its falling leaves and things.
The winding-down and muted colours that the changing season brings.
I love the freshness of the Spring; Nature's re-awakening.
Surely beyond the ken too far
to resist Spring's tra-la-la.

So, seasonal soliloquizing spent.
Soliloquizer seemingly seasonally content.

Royal British Legion Poppy Appeal

Residents at Deanland donated £431.46

Many Thanks for your support.

IS IT?

Sun was shining, sky was blue.
Birdsong filled the air.
Perce felt good!
Sprang from bed and flung
the window wide as e'er
  he could.
From the kitchen came the
  tantalising smell of bacon frying.
Percy quickly showered
  and donned his gear.
Oh, he was a happy man, of
  that there's no denying.
Run downstairs to share the
  day with those he held most dear.
Bonny children, pretty wife.
Puppy wagged his tail to greet.
Pussy curled around his feet.
Flowers on the window cill,
  roses round the door.
Perce thought, 'whatever <u>bliss</u> is,
  <u>this</u> is. Who could ask for more?
Now, I do not know Percy, or his family, puss or pup.
But it's grey outside, with <u>pouring</u> rain,
So I <u>conjured</u> them, to cheer things up.

                - - -

        Make-believe isn't lying,
           <u>Is</u> it?

IDLE IDYLL

I'd had my luncheon and dessert.
Well, - sandwich and a cup of tea
And thought, a little relaxation
wouldn't hurt.
In fact, be 'just the job' for me.
Talking of jobs, I'd <u>done</u> the chores.
The ones that <u>mattered</u> anyway.
So thought a little spell outdoors
would make my day.

And did it? Well you must believe
I won't keep it up my sleeve
When I settled in that chair, in
the sunny open-air.
Flowers blooming all around.
Sweet birdsong the only sound,
'twas wonderful beyond compare.
Closed my eyes and let myself
drift into joy's domain.
And might I say, if I have my way,
<u>tomorrow I'll do the same again</u>.

ARTISTIC LICENSE

When the sun sinks in the West.
That's where it goes, I'm told.
A lethargy comes over me, and a
  disembodied entity whispers in my ear
  "That's 'cos you're <u>old</u>."
Well, that's a fact I can't deny,
  and wouldn't even want to try.
For <u>old</u>, in its best moments, is a time of
  blameless leisure,
    with, oh, so many memories to treasure.

Were life a painter's palette, I would
choose these hues:
  Green for childhood, pink for youth,
  yellow for mature and gold for old.
Maybe I am prejudiced; I'm <u>pre</u> most everything,
  and when walking, even 'sleeping-
  policemen' pose a sort of dare.
But here's a little truism which may
  fit in somewhere:
'Whichever stage of life one's in,
  one's lucky to be there.'

Oh, I see the sun is setting,
  so I'd better soon be getting
    settled once again, in my armchair.

.

THAT DAY AGAIN

Near midnight: Little ones abed and fast asleep.
  But, oh what a task indeed it was - coaxing them
  counting sheep.
Teenage son is preening and playing 'Jack the lad'.
  Could be because the lass next door is
  here with her Mum and Dad.
The fairy-lights on the tree shine on the
  presents heaped below. But their sparkle
  will be well outshone with the children's eyes
  and faces all aglow.
Outside, the snow is snowing. Has been
  doing so all day. Setting the proper scene,
  no doubt, for Santa and his sleigh.
Festive fare all prepared. Well, as much
  as one can do. And dad has got the 'drinks'
  side sorted too.
Carol-singers are long gone; sweet echoes
  left behind. Their holy message lingering
  on the mind.
The mantel-clock strikes out the hour.
Twelve chimes, loud and clear.
Turn around. Well - I'll be bound.
- - Christmas Day is here!
  - - <u>Have a happy one</u>.

SING A SONG   2014

If you wake up in the morning
  and another hour, or two, of sleep
  is the thing for which you long,
Before you start your daily labours
- And don't live too near
  your neighbours,
- - Sing a song
If friends have upped and left
  and you feel a bit bereft,
Don't just sit around and mope
  that would be wrong!
Tell yourself you're
  all right Jack,
If they're true friends
  they'll be back
And - - Sing a Song
If Lady Luck seems to desert you
  do not let the parting hurt you
Just tell yourself that very soon
  good times will come along.
And if they take their time
  in coming,
Just try a little humming
- - Sing a song
Everyone knows that laughter
  is a gateway to good health.
But when you've gone through
  all the jokes that you can tell yourself
Just open up those vocal chords
  and make the rafters ring.
For, just like laughter,
  it is very good for you to sing.

THE CUP WINNER

My friend Irene, on a hobby-horse
Is hard to stop, when she's on course.
She was holding forth about the spring;
  its gentle charms and everything.

Tender seedlings peeping through,
Everything so fresh and new.
Emerald grass sparkling with dew.
Pastel blossom on the trees.
Lambs cavorting round the ewe.
The pale blue sky and balmy breeze.

I said, "Don't you think you're a
  bit old for Spring Fever?"
She said, "To value Nature? – <u>Never</u>!"
Who could disagree?

I said, "Let's have a cup of tea."
"To <u>Spring</u>!" She cried,
  clinking her cup against mine.
'*Crack!*' – a chill ran down my spine.
It was <u>good</u> china too,
  or <u>had</u> been, in its time.

I was about to remonstrate,
but realised, before too late,
that <u>no</u> potter, however clever,
or however keen, could cast
a mould that would compare
with my companion sitting there
 - my 'old china', Irene.

I smiled at her and to sum up,
  we had ourselves another cup.

TOMORROW SOUNDS GOOD

I've always been a ditherer,
   even when I was young.
Whenever in a quandary
   the same old song was sung.

Will I, won't I? Shall I or shan't I?
Shilly-shally Sally should
   have been my name.
And now that I am old, I fear
   my shilly-shallying's more severe
   and that little yellow streak has
   staked its claim.

I'm not <u>really</u> a coward,
   I, to myself declare.
It's just that differing opinions
   make me wish I wasn't there.
I don't want to be part of it
   should things go all askew.
Not right in the heart of it - -
Would you?

Perhaps you would,
   but you're not <u>me</u>.
So if controversy I see,
   I tell my friends with studied sorrow,
"Well goodbye then, -- see you tomorrow."
Coward?   Brave enough to tell <u>you</u> though.
Oh, - - I don't know - - - !!

KEEP ON KEEPING FIT

When they said, "Why don't you join 'Keep Fit'?"
I thought that they were bluffing.
The stage of fitness that I'd reached,
Is known as '<u>Fit for Nothing</u>'.
I thought, I can't raise high my arms,
Hadn't tried to for a while.
My heart was filled with wild alarms
Why, - I couldn't even raise a smile.
They said, "There's no need to fret,
- You just do what you can."
I thought, they haven't seen me yet,
- The classic <u>also-ran</u>.
I said, "I've come to Deanland
To live out my days at ease.
To rest and reminisce,
- Enjoy the flowers and the trees.
But, anyway, I went along
- In the morning, on a Tuesday.
And, would you believe,
- They were not wrong.
Tuesday, was my good news day.
A little stretching here and there,
A little bending too.
Before too long – I tell no lies
- I felt as good as new.

Creaking joints – forget them.
Aching arms – don't let them.
There really is no doubt of it
- The finest tonic is – 'Keep Fit'.

[PS Am a very old woman now.
Maybe wouldn't have made it thus far
Without 'Keep Fit', so - - - my thanks!]

SO THE DAY

As the gathering dusk of evening
folds its wings to close the day.
And the stars begin to cluster
in the heavens far away.
As the moon recoups its radiance,
and the hush of night-time sighs.
And my weary head, with gratitude,
upon the pillow lies.
As the blessings of the parting day
drift easy through the mind,
and pleasing thoughts of
passing hours unwind.
As my eyelids droop in slumber,
so my lips curve in a smile.
For I know, with God's grace,
there will be
another lovely day to see,
in just a little while.

SANTA FOR EVER

When I was young my stocking
hung, along with all the others.
Stockings empty yet, - before he
came.
That's right, - Santa is his name.
And yet already filled, it seems,
with all the childhood hopes and
dreams of me, my sisters and my
brothers.
And, oh, they were such shining
hours as breathlessly we waited.
Too excited far for sleep, you bet.
Struggling to stay awake, - and yet,
we never did achieve our aim,
to see him when he came.
As years went by, as they always do,
the Christmas picture altered too.
Speaking personally, it was
food and wine that became a preference
of mine.
Nowadays I still, of course,
enjoy the festive fun.
The holiness, the happiness, it
brings to everyone.
And hope and pray that every child
will be filled with delight.
And have a gift from that man in
Red with flowing beard so white.
For in this life a fantasy is
something of real worth.
So, may the fantasy survive, and keep
dear Santa Claus alive for everyone on earth.

- Happy Christmas!

THE BIRDSONG WAS SWEET   2015

They were in a sunlit garden
The old woman and the boy.
She on a comfy cushioned seat,
He with a favoured toy.
And birdsong was sweet,
From a nearby tree.

"Can I ask you something, Great Grandma?"
The boy said, in a while.
"Of course - what do you want to know?"
She answered, with a smile.
"Great Gran - why is your hair so white,
And the book you are reading held so near?"

The old lady thought for a little while,
And then she answered with a smile.
"When I was young, my hair was brown,
And my eyes were bright and clear."

He looked uncertain for a space
But then said with a serious face,
"Yes, – but, – why?"
Then he said, "And is it true,
That when you want to walk,
You find it really hard to <u>do</u>?"

His Gt. Gran smiled, then gave a sigh.
"You'll understand, dear, – by-and-by.
But not for a long, long time to come.
Till childhood's passed and youth has gone.
Till your dearest dreams have all come true,
And life's great gifts been known to you."

Cont...

"Have <u>you</u> done that then Great Grandma?
<u>Has</u> life been kind to <u>you</u>?"
The old lady's smile was pensive,
But the fervour in her voice rang true.
"Life has indeed been kind to me,
In many and many a way.
But - <u>best</u> of all, it gave me <u>you</u>."
The little boy laughed,
Then ran off to play.

And birdsong was sweet,
In the nearby tree - that day.

Hearing Aid Maintenance & Batteries

FREE SERVICE FOR NHS HEARING AIDS

At Deanland Social Centre
"Pop In"
From 10.00 - 12.00 noon
On : First Saturday of each month

Service provided by East Sussex Hearing Resource Centre
Telephone 01323 722505

www.eshrc.org.uk
Registered Charity No 1101140

AND I AM

Though in the winter of my years, - at nudging 98,
I kid myself it's not too late, or even inappropriate,
To appreciate the splendours of the spring.
Enjoy the softening of the breeze.
Admire the blossom on the trees.

Be glad to hear the rustling in the hedgerows down the lane,
As myriad tiny creatures wake and reclaim their domain.
Reminisce how, long ago, one too could leap and dance,
As the happy new-born lambs are wont to do.
And no-one can gainsay
That one's mind might sometimes stray
And let long-since memories of sweet
Springtime romance come drifting through.

Maybe I cling too tightly to the wonders of the world,
And should submit that I have had my fling.
But, whilst I am still here, it really seems quite clear
That everyone, be old or young,
When the wondrous spring has sprung,
Can only be delighted that it's here.

And I Am

WILL YOU?

Will you come with me down to the shore,
  as we used in the balmy days of yore?
And watch the waves and smell the sea,
  in the place where love blossomed
  for you and me.
When we were young and our
  unsuspecting hearts were free.
On that golden, enchanted, moonlit beach,
  where the very stars seemed
  within our reach.

<u>Will</u> you? - My love of so many years.
Soulmate in hopes and dreams and fears.
Will you tryst with me, as in days gone by?
Hands close-clasped 'neath the starry sky.
Will you come with me, so that we may,
  together stand on that sea drenched sand?
And drift back through the years
  to our wedding day?
    - <u>Will</u> you?

TO BE FRANK

There are two sorts of surprises:
Nice, and the other kind.
Frank afforded one of each that I can bring to mind.
He had a little news-stand on a busy London street.
"All the news; all the latest," he would cry,
To catch the ears of passers-by.
Buying my daily paper, if things were quiet, we'd chat
About the latest headlines, say, or bits of this and that.

The photo fixed to the news-stand -
That was the first surprise;
and certainly not the <u>nice</u> one.
I felt tears cloud my eyes.
Frank! An army-officer, bemedalled and erect.
He shrugged. "It's not, I s'pose, what you'd expect.
But you know what they say –
When you reach rock bottom,
<u>Up</u> is the only way."
He put his hand to his forehead;
in a quasi military salute.
Then turned to his next customer as if he
didn't give a hoot.

I walked on; saddened and maddened.
Circumstances took me from the area,
but several months later,
In the West End, Frank's second surprise,
I hardly believed my eyes.
It was nice, nice, nice!
He was standing beside a gleaming limousine.
Prosperous-looking and serene.
Smiling, he gave me that quasi salute;
Stepped into the car and was away.
What can I say! I <u>had</u> to go back,
Back to the East End. <u>Had</u> to <u>see</u>, to be <u>sure</u>!
Frank wasn't at the news-stand any more.
The new chap must have wondered at my smug
and beaming smile.
It didn't fade for quite a while
– to be frank.

FARES PLEASE

Meg overslept and missed her bus;
So had to walk to work.
And that is when, it turned out,
Fate staged a little quirk.
For that's the day when Meg met Vince.
They <u>collided</u>, she confided
And he's been with her ever since.
Their future was decided.
She told him she had missed her bus.
He smiled and said, "Fares please."
She grinned; said, "You'd be lucky."
He gave her hand squeeze.
And do you know in just a while,
They were side-by-side along the aisle.
And, in their life together,
Fair or foul the weather,
If little difficulties evolved
Domestic problems to be solved
Smiling at her, "Fares please" he'd say,
And troubles seemed to fade away.
When, with a baby on her knees
Vince murmured, "<u>Look</u> at <u>us</u>."
Meg smiled, and whispered back, "Fares please."
And blessed the day she'd missed that bus.

OH! AND HO-HO-HO!

Oh, - the glistening holly and beguiling mistletoe.
Is the young lass waiting there to claim her
favourite beau?
Will the old lady with lines down her cheek
Gain a kiss from the old chap that makes her
knees weak?
Will the mums and dads queue up for their turn
and be lost in a kiss that will make their cheeks burn?
Will the toddlers' imploring arms beg for their go?
Of course! – Because it's Christmas! – Ho-ho-ho!

And, oh! – There's magic everywhere.
Even before Santa's booming, "Ho-ho-ho" floats
across the frosty air.
And, oh! – The presents and the carols and the fun.
And that special festive feeling that lays claim to everyone.
Oh! – The happy greetings as friends and families gather,
Warming the cockles of one's heart however cold
the weather.
Oh-oh-oh! – It's wonderful; the goodwill and the fun.
And, - Ho-ho-ho! – The sleigh bells!
Santa's <u>here</u>! He's <u>really</u> come!
<u>Oh</u>, yes! – A <u>very</u>, <u>very</u> Merry Christmas, everyone.

BLIND DATE (Pre Internet) 2016

Madge had found him as a pen-friend in a magazine,
And things had sort of followed on from there.
They seemed of very similar minds in the letters they'd exchanged.
And now he had suggested that a meeting be arranged.
Asked if she would like to, and, if so, when and where?

Now Madge was nervous as a cat.
She hadn't quite expected that.
He'd told her he was tall and slim
And that his hair was dark.
She'd written back and said she'd meet him in the park.
But now the nerves! My word!
Tall & slim? Like a beanpole?
And <u>Mephistopheles</u> was dark, so she had heard.

What have I done? Madge asked herself.
What have I begun?
I'm in a state. My first Blind Date.
Well, I can just go there and see.
Then, if I'm sure he's not for me,
I can <u>flee</u>.

But wait, let's just give this a chance,
Might be my heart's desire.
A truly heaven-sent romance,
For which all girls aspire.
The ship of life is crewed by 3.
Man & maid & Fate.

He could be fun.
Could be the <u>one</u>.
Hurrah for this Blind Date.

OH, MAVE!

I said to my friend Mavis, "It's spring, so raise a smile"
She looked at me; I thought I glimpsed a tear.
I said, "Mavis, - what's the matter?
You're generally overboard with rapture
as soon as the first crocuses appear."

She shrugged, and turned her head away.
I didn't know quite what to say.
Then ventured, "Mavis, is there something wrong?
You can tell me, - I won't blab."
She said, "I know, - you're my best friend."
- then gave her eyes a dab.
I said "Well - what is it all about?
Maybe we can sort it out."

She said, "You know that Charlie Jones
I've been out with once or twice?"
I said, "I do, - I think he's very nice"
She said, "He's very good to me, and I
really love his company, but ---------"
"But what?"
"The other day I saw him with a woman on his arm,
and I must say it's bothering me a lot."

I grinned. She wept. Then in I leapt.
"Oh, Mave, - that is his sister-in-law.
His younger brother's wife.
I met them at the shops the other day.
They're on a family visit for just a little stay;
So put that silly handkerchief away."

Cont...

Mavis pulled a face at me, then said, with dancing eyes, and arms flung wide in a worldwide embrace, "Hey, - don't you realise it's Spring? Look at the buds and everything.
Smell the fragrance in the air.
The soft breeze on your face.
The new life starting everywhere."

I smiled as we sauntered on, along a leafy lane.
All that just brought home to me what I'd known from the start.
Though there is winter in Mave's years,
Nothing can quench the springtime in her heart.
    Tears gone. Spring's won. - - Again!!

JUST JESS

Jess lives in a cottage, close beside a stream,
In a pretty little tree-lined glade,
Bordering a village set around a green,
Where all of those who know her
Hold Jess in high esteem.
A dog called Joe and a cat called Min,
Complete her home, when they're all in.
Jess gathers herbs and mushrooms
And eggs from the hens she keeps.
She tends weak or wounded creatures,
And for their plight she weeps.

                                                                  Cont.

Jess is an early riser; sometimes before the dawn,
For she loves to watch the sun rise through the trees.
And the beauty of the glade in early morning mist,
Jess finds, is just too tempting to resist.
Children gather round her to voice their joys and woes,
And gain the praise or sympathy required.
And grown-ups too, it seems, should mishap befall,
Tend to make the cottage in the glade, first port of call!
Those whom age or circumstance has rendered 'not so able'
Oft find delicacies Jess has made embellishing their table.

Sociable and fun-loving; always a joy to see.
Her many friends ensure that Jess is seldom short of company.
At close of day, hens locked away; the setting sun,
The vivid sky; the homing birds as they drift by;
The silence, calm & deep, are balm
To Jess's grateful soul, ere she succumbs to sleep.

I must confess I'm proud of Jess, and to write of her a boon.
But she is fiction, I'm afraid.
Though there are such as she around,
And, who knows, one could well be found,
Living in a cottage close beside a stream,
In a pretty little tree-lined glade.
    -- Maybe soon!

SO IT'S SUMMER

Someone with a paint-brush has shaded out the clouds,
   and lavished on the sky a deeper blue.
Up in the trees the birds are on what seems a festive spree.
   Twittering and hopping and singing joyously.
Meadows are emblazoned with buttercups and daisies,
   and the painter's been there too, with emerald green.
Myriad blossoms everywhere;
   their fragrance lingering in the air.
Everybody seems to be light-hearted and at ease;
   whilst the radiant sun smiles smugly at his mega
   power to please.
Roses; strawberries and cream. Days out by the shore.
   Cool drinks in the garden. Who could ask for more?

   So! it's Summer!!

FROWN?

"Are you unhappy, Irene? Has something got you down?
I must admit it's rare to see you frown."
"Oh, - was I frowning, Mary? I can't imagine why.
Perhaps I will remember if I try.
Well, - let me see. - I woke up late this morning - but I don't
think it's that; for a little hasting, got things back on line.
Besides, the extra forty-winks was fine.
Oh, and the toaster played me up, but I managed with the grill,
and I think the toast tastes better in a way.
No, I don't think <u>that</u> caused grief, I have to say.
Oh, when I was hurrying, I dropped a cup of tea,
but didn't crack the cup, and a mop soon cleaned that up.
So, no, - I don't think that caused too much bother. You know,
I really can't pin down what could have caused my frown.
Oh, the kitchen sink got clogged, but Bob cleared that in a tick, -
so <u>that</u> was not the cause for woe at all.
Of course, getting up late made a race to get the kids to school on
time, but we made it, so that really turned out fine. No, Mary,
though I try, I really cannot figure why there's any simple reason
for the frown.
I'm really very happy that's all that I can say.
Oh, I've just remembered, - when I dropped the cup of tea,
I tripped up on the mat and got entangled with the cat,
but he gave a little spit and ran out of my way,
so that was just a little slip. OK?
Sister dear, now <u>you</u> are frowning. You must know I'm only
clowning; so put your sunny smile back right away.
Here, - let me take your arm."
Two smiling sisters, full of charm;
off to spend a lovely day in town.
And, heaven forfend a frown!

SEASONAL GREETINGS

Can't believe it's here again.
The fairy lights and fun.
The cards and invitations.
The endless lists of this and that,
Which simply must be done
The pantomimes and school plays.
The shopping and the chores.
We're busy, but we love it all -
Because, - - It's Christmas!!

And at the very heart of it
We're still following that
Guiding star which led us to the
Holy birth and the sanctity of
Christmas here on earth.

The joyful ringing of the bells,
The carol-singing choirs.
The happy eyes of children as
They tender their desires.
The heart-warming festive season
Nullifies frost and snow.
So have a lovely Christmas,
Ho – ho – ho!

DREAM ON

2017

The other night I tossed and turned.
Just couldn't get to sleep.
But when at last I did, it was to dream.
And such a dream; worth waiting for.
It filled my heart with joy.
Memories upon memories
Seemed to strive for space.
Vying with each other for a place.

The many years I've lived have fostered
Multi-memories.
Not <u>all</u> of them sublime, but mostly so.
And the dreams selected for me,
As if aiming to be kind, were the loveliest moments
In my life that could be brought to mind.

I woke refreshed & light of heart
To face the new-born day.
For, though dreams, as is their wont,
Had drifted on their way,
The happiness I'd garnered,
Chose graciously to stay.

This is a will-o'-the-wisp account,
As dreams can only be,
But, after all is said and done,
I'll find no cause to wail or weep,
When, at the setting of the sun,
Should kindly dream-makers prevail,
I lay me down to sleep,
   - And dream on!

SPRINGS TO MIND

Don't you just love the coming of the spring?
The sense of new beginnings that the season
 seems to bring?
To me, it seems a time of *'ations'*. Expect*ation*;
 anticip*ation*; re-cre*ation*.

How pleasing to hear the twittering of the birds
 as they re-line their nests.
The cheeping of chicks as tiny lungs are put
 to pensive test.

The sheer determin*ation* of the crocuses and such
 as they thrust for all their worth, through the
 winter-hardened earth, to endow us with
 the bold display that we enjoy so much.

The realis*ation* that life, like nature,
 always gives new chance.
That seeming lost ambitions
 can invite another glance.

That is the message of the spring.
A fresh approach to everything.

   So, -- -- enjoy!

PENSIVE PEGGY

They called her 'Pensive Peggy'.
She was often deep in thought.
Sometimes even in a crowded room.
When they saw that far-away look in her smiling eyes
Those who were her closest friends could always realise,
"She's gone," they'd whisper, behind a hand,
"Off to Never Never Land."

From being a 'leading light,' quite suddenly she might
Withdraw, just like a shadow in the night.
At first her friends were curious.
Whatever could the matter be?
But finally they told themselves,
"She's re-charging her battery".

One day a handsome stranger sauntered through the door.
Romance blossomed, as well it may.
And on her Wedding Day Peg said,
"Man of my dreams. No need to day-dream anymore."
One or two of her friends, though,
Thought that they'd 'give it a go'.
For who knows all the 'ifs' and 'mights'
And who that angel with the arrows
May have in his sights.

Oh, I'm sorry. Please excuse,
Must just have a little snooze.

Space For More Poems – Hopefully.

Space For More Poems – Hopefully.

AND FINALLY . . . ?

March 2017

As well as these *News* poems, Doris has written many more for her personal pleasure. Others were written for special occasions or to meet requests from friends and family. Doris has also written a very moving account her younger years.

Born in Shoreditch during a First World War air raid, she lived there until she was eighteen. Doris was the middle child of seven, four brothers and two sisters. Her account tells of the trials and tribulations as well as the fun and joy of the inter-war years.

The family of nine lived in a two bedroom flat off Great Eastern Street. It was part of a block of purpose built Victorian flats, know as Hamilton Buildings. Although crowded, it seems as though they all coped remarkably well, helped, no doubt, by the well equipped accommodation.

As well as the two bedrooms (one for the boys and one for the parents and girls), they had a large 'front room', with coal fire, a kitchen and a balcony. The kitchen had a 'Butler's' sink and cold tap, a coal-fired range, a coal-fired 'copper' (for clothes washing), a gas stove and a coal store under the draining board. All lit by gas mantles.

The balcony, just outside the kitchen, was a particularly useful feature as this had the 'privy' (with torn up newspaper), a space to hang the galvanised bath and a rubbish chute down to the basement store.

Doris' account is justifiably full of praise for her parents, who raised a large family in constrained surroundings and through two World Wars.

Doris celebrated her 99th birthday in July 2016 and in spite of her protestations that she will not make her 100th, the whole family are convinced that she will. Her cake-baking niece, who lives in France, is already planning both the cake and the trip to Deanland. 'Watch this space'!

Doris and Stephen
about to enjoy lunch at
The Inn on the Park

2017 has also proved significant in the history of Deanland as the family that has owned & run the park since 1954, announced that they had sold the company that owns the site.

What this will mean to the many residents remains to be seen – or 'Watch this space' too!

Retirement of the family that owns the Park   *News* item Dec 2016

The Park has been in the same family ownership since 1954, the ownership passed to the second generation headed by the current Managing Director, Keith Whitehead, who started in the family business in 1963. The other owners are, Tanya Head, Nigel Wolek and Richard Whitehead, who lives in Australia.

Keith tried retirement some years ago, but could not let go, going to the office every day. This situation was not helped by living very close to the Park in the "manager's bungalow"

It is now time for him to properly retire, for this to work he has to move and together with the rest of the family, has taken the opportunity to sell all their shares in the Park.

Keith's son Steve has been the Park Manager for some 12 years and is staying on for a while, as is Jennie. This is good news as they work very well together as a team.

The Inn on the Park will be managed, not by Deanland Wood Park as it is now, but by Debbie Toms who will run it under a Management Agreement, so the trading of the Inn will be her own business.

It is important to realise that the residents of the Park will be unaffected as all the Agreements are with Deanland Wood Park Ltd., so remain valid, as it is the shareholders in Deanland Wood Park that is changing.

The new owner of the shares is Mr John Sargeant, who is an experienced Park owner with several Parks in the Surrey area. Deanland should fit in nicely with his organisation.

A personal note from Keith Whitehead

I have thoroughly enjoyed my time at Deanland Park; I have met some very good friends, who I hope will remain so into the future. Our staff has been our real strength and I thank them all for their loyal and long term service, I shall miss them all.

I have known many people and seen many changes of the years, there has been many "characters" that have left a lasting impression. I feel comfortable that the Park and its residents are in good hands.

I hope to be able to come back occasionally to have a drink with these good friends.

I wish you all good health and happiness for the future and a very Merry Christmas and a great New Year.

Keith

Made in the USA
Columbia, SC
09 June 2017